More on *Grace and Holiness in a Changing World:*

"This thought-provoking and deeply insightful book will capture your attention in its introduction and continue to grip you until the last page. I found myself wishing every clergy and layperson in the church could come to know and incorporate the truths revealed by the authors of these writings. These understandings are core for the twenty-first century Christian who yearns to join God in reaching out to this new world."

—Alfred W. Gwinn Jr., Resident Bishop
Raleigh Episcopal Area, The United Methodist Church

"*Grace and Holiness in a Changing World: A Wesleyan Proposal for Postmodern Ministry* by Dr. Greenway and Dr. Joel Green is a wonderful addition to the ongoing conversation in the church about what it means to have a twenty-first century ministry consistent with our Wesleyan tradition. For those of us who seek to apply our Wesleyan heritage to the cultural challenges around us, this book will prove to be of tremendous help. The more we understand the historical context in which we live and critique it through our Wesleyan lens, the more we will continue to see God's renewing and reforming work in the world and the Church."

—G. Lindsey Davis, Resident Bishop
North Georgia Episcopal Area, The United Methodist Church

"Christianity has always been counterculture, whether in its pre-modernity infancy or in this postmodern world. *Grace and Holiness in a Changing World* gives proof that the gospel is ever relevant and why the church must never surrender to culture but always speak with grace and truth."

—Dr. Frederick J. Finks, President, Ashland Theological Seminary

Grace and Holiness in a Changing World

A Wesleyan Proposal for Postmodern Ministry

JEFFREY E. GREENWAY
JOEL B. GREEN

Abingdon Press
Nashville

Library of Congress Cataloging-in-Publication Data

Grace and holiness in a changing world : a Wesleyan proposal for postmodern ministry / edited by Jeffrey E. Greenway and Joel B. Green.
    p. cm.
Includes bibliographical references.
ISBN-13: 978-0-687-46570-5 (pbk. : alk. paper)
    1. Methodist Church—Doctrines. 2. Wesley, John, 1703–1791. 3. Postmodernism—Religious aspects—Christianity. 4. Theology, Doctrinal. 5. Pastoral theology. 6. Church work. I. Greenway, Jeffrey E., 1960– II. Green, Joel B., 1956–

BX8331.3.G73 2007
230'.7--dc22
                                                                    2006028820

07 08 09 10 11 12 13 14 15 16—10 9 8 7 6 5 4 3 2 1

MANUFACTURED IN THE UNITED STATES OF AMERICA

CONTENTS

IN RESPONSE TO GRACE

Jeffrey E. Greenway

Would you agree with me? The world we live in is in a tremendous state of flux:

- The lines that were drawn by the cold war of the last half of the twentieth century have been erased, and the global community is in a constant state of change.
- The cultural definitions of Christendom and modernity have passed by in the landscape of time, and the culture around us reflects the signs and symptoms of postmodernity, with all of its ambiguity.
- In some circles, truth has become an exercise in relativity.
- The "family" has come to mean many different things to many different people. Divorce is on the rise. Marriage seems to be a passing convenience. Single parents and their children are feeling the stresses and strains of these days and times.
- Families are increasingly stressed by diminishment of resources. Parents often hold two or three jobs in an effort to live at the standard that was common in their formative years.

- *Working poor* has become a socioeconomic category that has an increasingly familiar face.
- Homelessness is a paycheck away for many individuals and families, and the social safety net for such persons has holes in it.
- The rise of terrorism as a means of disruption and influence reaches into previously unthinkable places, like schools, and the impact frays the fabric of peace and stability.
- Human effort to root out "evil" has proved to be unsuccessful, and it is becoming increasingly clear that there are some problems that cannot be solved by force or diplomacy, but only by the reconciling work of Jesus on the cross.
- The world's peoples have a growing population of have-nots who are becoming increasingly impatient and angry with those who have, which reminds us that recent unrest in the world is a foretaste of what may be—unless something happens to spread the limited resources of our planet around.
- Our planet is showing the effects of creation's being treated like a garbage dump for the last century, and the signs and symptoms of this abuse are startling.
- Human life continues to decrease in value. The elderly are put away as an afterthought. Children are the victims of violence that was unthinkable a generation ago. The sweatshops that were outlawed in the West have moved to a different climate and culture. The global economy is often built on the backs of, and through the exploitation of, those in developing countries who do not have a voice. And babies continue to be aborted with the same lack of conscience with which they were conceived.

The world is dramatically changing. What a great time to be a Wesleyan Christian!

We want to share what grace and holiness in the Wesleyan tradition mean in this era. For my part, I am sharing four thoughts for your consideration as you seek to be a spiritual leader in the world and times in which we find ourselves. They are: "Our Mission," "Our Milieu," "Our Message," and "Our Model."

Our Mission

The church of Jesus Christ is the hope of the world, if and only if we remember our mission. The church's mission is to make disciples of Jesus Christ. We are to be an aid station where people who are hurting in this world can come and find compassion from those around them. We are to be a saving station, where people who come into our midst will encounter the living Christ and want to live in response to the saving grace he offers to us. We are to be a filling station where disciples of Jesus come, are taught the Scriptures, are nurtured to mature discipleship, have the character of Christ formed in them, are filled with the Holy Spirit, and discover and use their gifts for ministry. We are to be a sending station that launches all of God's people in mission and ministry, not just within the walls of the church, but in the communities and in the world, in a Jerusalem-Judea-Samaria-uttermost-parts-of-the-earth kind of way. The church does not exist for itself or its members. The church exists for the lost and lonely, the hurting and humiliated, the desperate and dying. The church is not a haven for saints who have "arrived." The church is a hospital for sinners who are "found" on the journey.

During the last five years, I have been a District Superintendent providing leadership to over 60 churches in the eastern half of Allegheny County in Pittsburgh, Pennsylvania. I observed that many of the congregations that I superintended had forgotten their mission. They had forgotten why God has strategically placed them in their communities. They had a sort of corporate amnesia when it came to their mission.

Some of them had become private clubs for members only and unless you knew the password or the secret handshake you would never be welcomed to enter. They paid their dues so they could park in their parking places and sit in their pews. Others had what Frank Tillepaugh called, in *Unleashing the Church*, a fortress mind-set.[1] They would say that they were friendly people—and they were, if you could swim the moat, climb the walls, and fight past the guards whom they called ushers—they were very friendly people. I found some of our congregations to be militarily defensible, and the attitudes of the people therein reflected that mentality. Some had become museums where every artifact of a former time was preserved, until perhaps Jesus might come again. The artifacts inside no longer reflected the community outside. Some of the congregations had become hospices. They would rather die than change, and they will, because they have forgotten their mission and purpose. A club, a fortress, a museum, a hospice—this is not what God placed those churches there to be.

Why do you think churches may become that way? At some point, their leaders and members developed corporate ecclesiastical amnesia. They forgot their mission. They failed to read the culture around them, and decided their fate. They failed to realize the times, context, and milieu in which they live, and to remember their mission, which is to offer Christ to people and give them the opportunity to live in response to grace.

Our Milieu

We live in an awesome time in history. Some sociologists have called it a crack in history, a seismic shift in culture that may happen only once or twice a millennium. It is happening right now. It is an incredible time of change and if the church does not recognize it, we will lose an opportunity and become a museum to an age gone by.

Most historians agree that there are four major periods of Christian history—only four in the nearly 2,000 years since the beginning of the church of Jesus Christ. The first, the *apostolic era*, began in A.D. 33 with the death, resurrection, and ascension of Jesus Christ, and the gift of the Holy Spirit being poured out on all flesh at Pentecost. It lasted for a little under 300 years until about A.D. 313. This is the period of time that we read about in the New Testament. This is the church in its earliest, most basic form. In the Bible and history, the church of this age is a minority sect, in a pluralistic, pagan culture.

To become a follower of Jesus in this era was a life-altering decision. Those early followers of Jesus often followed him at great risk, and martyrdom was common. The ministry emphasis of the early church was a holistic form of evangelism. Billy Abraham has described this as "the process of initiating people into the Kingdom of God."[2] There is strong evidence of personal and corporate evangelism, catechesis (or disciple making), distribution of spiritual gifts among the followers of Jesus for mission and ministry, and engaging the entire body of Christ in its primary mission of making disciples. The apostolic church was formed around the priesthood of all believers: the *laos*, the whole people of God.

The apostolic church was more an organism than it was an organization. Although there is some reference in the New Testament to deacons, elders, and even bishops, it does not seem to be structure-oriented, but rather leadership-oriented, in order to align the church's use of the gifts of ministry for the rest of the body of Christ. (See Ephesians 4.)

Doctrine mattered in this era of the church: there is clear evidence of the codification of core doctrines of the Christian faith, and that these doctrines were taught to the followers of the risen Jesus.

The apostolic church was a first-generation church. It recognized that the reason it existed was to introduce people to the risen Jesus, to disciple them in his name, to help them to receive the Holy Spirit, and to send them out so they might be able to reach other people and introduce them to the risen Jesus and do the very same thing. This was a contagious, evangelistic, disciple-making, mission-hearted community of faith. That is the kind of church we read about in the New Testament.

The second major era of the Christian faith, called the *Christendom Era*, started around A.D. 313 when Constantine was converted to Christ. In the ensuing 1,400 years, Christianity became more socially mainstream and eventually became the state religion. Church and state began to function as one and the same. The church was the primary shaper of the mores of the culture. As Christianity became more and more mainstream, the emphasis on evangelism and disciple making began to wane. Persons did not become Christians because they left a former way of life to join a countercultural movement. They became Christians because they were born into that Christendom culture.

The church began to move away from the Great Commission mission as described in the New Testament, and toward a codification and ritualization of the Christian life from cradle to grave. In the Christendom tradition, seven different sacraments were developed to mark the journey from cradle to grave: baptism, confession, communion, confirmation, marriage, ordination, and last rites.

During this era, the Christian church became institutionalized. Cathedrals were built. Administrative structures to preserve the institution were developed. The church developed a highly sophisticated stratification of clergy leadership with less emphasis placed upon the priesthood of all believers. Spiritual gifts are rarely mentioned in the writing of this era. Pastor/priests become the mediators of all grace, and held the functions of ministry within their office. They become the sole interpreters of Scripture and dispensers of grace through the sacraments. The work of the people, the *laos*, was relegated to attending worship, giving the offering, receiving the sacraments, and doing the liturgy of the church. The foundational doctrines of the apostolic era began to be interpreted and codified into the dogma of the Christendom church.

Christendom became a social, economic, and political way of life with church and state working hand in hand. (If you drive through middle America, you can see a clear sign of the residue of Christendom. When you go to a county seat, look at the town square. On one end of the town square will be the county courthouse. What is on the other end? A church. And if you research the history of that town, the players in the county courthouse were also the players in that church. The pastor of that congregation was often the most influential person in that community. Church and state functioned together. They determined what happened in that community: church and state, working together, Christendom at its best.)

One of the challenges we face these days is that we have trained leaders to function as if this Christendom reality were still true, and it is not.

The third era of Christian history is the *Modern/Enlightenment Era*. It started about 1750 with the rise of the Industrial Revolution and the Academy. At the beginning of this era church and state worked together, as is evidenced in Wesley's England and the early history of the United States. But as the Enlightenment began to take root, skepticism and rationalism flourished and began to call the doctrines and dogmas of the Christendom era into question. Eventually, the church began to lose its sway over the state.

Skepticism also altered the way many viewed the Scriptures. The authority of Scripture was compromised. The miracles were questioned. The sinful condition of humanity was rationalized. The divinity and resurrection of Jesus were diminished to a fable. The result? Without the authority of Scripture and the divinity of Jesus, without the power and reality of the resurrection, the Christian faith of the Enlightenment became a collection of moral teachings that, to paraphrase the words of Wesley, had the form of religion, but lacked the power.[3]

The Academy was complicit in this skepticism. It began to question whether the foundations of our faith were true, and as that became the norm, the church began to lose standing in the culture. As a result, for the last 200 years the church of Jesus has been an institutional organization in survival mode, rather than a vital organism.

We can identify some notable exceptions to this prevailing view: the Wesleyan Revival and late-nineteenth-century Evangelicalism, for example; but the norm was a Christian faith that had all the form of religion, but lacked the power.

That leads me to the fourth era of Christian faith: the *postmodern era.* I believe this is the era we are living in right now. It started somewhere in the last fifty years. Most people cannot tell exactly when it started, but we can say something about what it looks like. It looks like the first century all over again. The Christian church, whether we choose to realize it or not, is once again a minority sect in a prevailingly pluralistic, pagan world culture. We want to function as if we are still living in the Christendom or Enlightenment eras, but this era we are living in right now is a post-Christendom, post-Enlightenment, postmodern era.

For the church to find its way in the future, the answer is in our past. We need to pick up the mantle of the apostolic church: to be distinctively who we are, to call people to life change and transformation, to become intentional about personal and corporate evangelism, to model catechesis (or disciple making), to emphasize the discovery and use of spiritual gifts among the followers of Jesus for mission and ministry, and to engage the whole people of God in the mission, of making disciples.

An amazing thing is happening today. It is almost as if God has pulled back the screen of Scripture and enabled us to rediscover spiritual gifts all over again. During the last couple of decades clergy leaders have begun to rise up and say, "I'm not the only one to do ministry here, but I'm to help you, to equip you, to do the work of ministry for building up the body of Christ in an Ephesians 4 manner." For the church to live and flourish in this era, it must once again become a countercultural movement. We are not supposed to look like the world. We are supposed to look different from the world and call people to a different kind of life.

Here is the problem: Culturally, the church is viewed as the minority sect of a pagan, pluralistic culture, but we keep trying to operate as through we live in Christendom. We spend all of our energy maintaining organizational structures rather than being an organism. We spend our energy trying to make members who become a part of our club rather than making disciples of Jesus Christ with a kingdom view. We train clergy leaders who hold power and see themselves as the sole dispensers of grace rather than as fellow pilgrims on the journey whose role is to call people to faith, to equip them for ministry, and to set them free to minister to others in Jesus' name.

If we would live we must remember what time it is. We are not in Christendom any more. The Enlightenment has run its course. Some may be dismayed about the milieu of this context, but not me. This is a great time to be a part of the kingdom. What a great time to be a Wesleyan Christian!

Our Message

Our message is grace. We are called to teach and model grace in the fullness of the Wesleyan tradition. Grace: prevenient, saving, assuring, perfecting, glorifying. Grace: we need to live it, teach it, preach it, model it, be transformed by it, and live in response to it.

To really get this, I believe we need a fresh understanding of what grace is. I had an epiphany moment at the 2004 General Conference of The United Methodist Church in Pittsburgh. We were in the throes of debate, and everyone (on all sides) was talking about grace. It occurred to me that we talk a lot about grace, but I do not think we really know what it is. We tend to lower grace to the lowest common denominator. We do not expect the life change that grace is because we bifurcate it from the holiness of God.

Grace is pretty amazing. We serve a God who will accept anyone where they are. But if that is all we preach we miss a very important part of the Wesleyan grace continuum. We need to preach the whole of grace: prevenient grace, saving grace, sanctifying grace, and living life in response to that grace until the time comes when we receive glorifying grace. This does not often happen in our churches. The reason I think we do not do that is because we have cheapened it over the years by separating it from the holiness of God. We cannot understand the depth of grace apart from the holiness of God.

In Isaiah 6, we find Isaiah in the temple. He sees the Lord. He encounters a holy God, and the Scripture tells us that he exclaims, "Woe is me! I am lost, for I am a man of unclean lips, and I live among a people of unclean lips" (v. 5). In that moment of naked vulnerability, Isaiah knew that God was holy and he was not. He was in the wrong place at the wrong time with a holy God.

I believe that picture is being painted in the first part of the second chapter of Ephesians. Paul is describing our condition: dead in our sins because we follow the prince of this world. We are a people in desperate need of grace.

Have you ever come face to face with the holiness of God and known that you are undone?

When I was a student at Asbury Theological Seminary, I remember hearing all the stories of conversion of my fellow students. Amazing stories! I had lived a pretty pedestrian life to that point. My son Joseph likes to call me a Boy Scout, because I did not drink or swear, smoke or chew, and I never dated the girls who did. I was a pretty ordinary guy: raised in a Christian home, practicing the holy habits of our faith from the time I can remember. I had made a decision to follow Jesus when I was thirteen. That was the way it was.

But when I came to Asbury, I entered an environment where the stories of grace were evident and I began to question my faith. I began to pray for what John Wesley called assurance of salvation. I remember the night that I encountered Jesus in a dream. Every cell in my body began to burn. And every bit of my being began to realize that I was in the presence of Someone who was holier than I, and I was undone. I still remember when I woke up from that dream I couldn't talk. My wife, Beth, was lying asleep in the bed next to me. I could not move my extremities. I lay there for an hour moving from fear of a righteous and holy God to dependence on the grace of God as the only one who could save me. God did a work in my heart that night. That was the night I came to know that assurance of my salvation, that God had saved me, even me, from my sin, and that I would live my life in response to that kind of saving grace.

A transition took place within me, because I experienced grace in the context of the holiness of God. When we understand the holiness of God and how awesome God is, what can we do? This is the God who created the heavens and the earth and the God who put the stars and mountains in place. When we understand the God who created us for his pleasure to be in relationship with him, what can we do? This is the God who knit us together inside of our mother's wombs and knows everything there is to know about us. This is the same God who from the fall has been putting into place the redemption of humanity, who loved us so much that he became one of us and lived with us and talked to us and prayed for us and healed us and died for us and rose for us. This God loves every one of us as if there were only one of us to love. When we come to realize that our holy God loves us in that way, the only thing we can do is surrender to grace by faith.

In Ephesians 2:8-10, Paul recognizes our need to feel as if we have to earn it, that there is something we can do to make this happen. That is where most of us get stuck. We try to earn grace, rather than receive it.

Sometimes, when I am talking about the need to accept grace by faith because we cannot do it on our own, I will invite a small child to come stand next to me. I will say, "Okay, we're going to jump to the moon this morning." On the count of three, we will jump. I then ask the congregation who jumped higher, and they will always say the child jumped higher than I did. But when it comes to jumping from the earth to the moon, does it matter? The chasm is so great that I could not possibly get there without help. That is the way our works are compared to the holiness of God. They are so lacking that we cannot span the chasm by our efforts. We need the grace of God to span the gap for us. We just have to accept that the grace of God will take us the rest of the way home. We are saved by grace through faith.

Living in response to grace starts with the holiness of God. It then proceeds to a grace transaction. In the story of Isaiah, the grace transaction comes after Isaiah exclaims, "Woe is me! . . . for I am a man of unclean lips, and I live among a people of unclean lips." An angel takes a hot coal off the altar and touches Isaiah's lips, cleansing him for God's purposes.

We also learn from these texts that our response to grace is holiness: holiness of heart and life. Ephesians 2:10 reminds us that, even though we are not saved by our works, we are created for them. The only good works we can do in response to grace is to live in holiness. Holiness is not just on the front end of the grace equation. Holiness is what flows out as authentic response. It is true: our holy God accepts us exactly where we are, at the lowest place we can come, but it is equally true that God loves us too much to leave us there. God wants us to become the people he had in mind when he first thought of creating us. And so the rest of our lives are lived in response to grace, so that we begin to reflect the holiness and the character of God to the people around us, so that God's grace might become so attractive that others will want to follow Jesus too. We are to be holy even as our Father in heaven is holy.

Holiness is not simply naming the sin in ourselves and others. It is discovering for ourselves and telling others what we have found to be right about Jesus and beginning to reflect his character in our lives. Holiness is not a laundry list of behaviors we are against as much as it is a reflection of the life of grace that calls us to become more like Jesus.

Many of the churches I have encountered have forgotten both ends of this grace transaction. They lower grace to this watered-down version of "do whatever you want," and God wants so much more of us than that. I am not calling us to return to the condemning time of past evangelicalism; I am calling us to look at Jesus and the early church and find the tender balance of naming sin and the brokenness it causes—while announcing grace and holiness; I am calling us to embrace all that we have found to be right about Jesus.

We need to reclaim a gracious call to repent from one way of life to follow another. When we repent, the word literally means that we turn 180 degrees from walking away from God; we turn our lives "God-ward" and walk back in that direction. The church is not always clear about this call. Many followers of Jesus stand there still facing in the same direction of our former lives, and God wants more for us than that. Beth and I have three children, they are twenty, eighteen, and sixteen years of age. When God gave them to us, they came just as they were. They could not do anything for themselves, and whatever they did do for themselves was a mess to be cleaned up. But we lovingly accepted them as they were, and we began to pour into that life and love and faith. And we began to teach them to clean up after themselves. We potty trained them, taught them to feed themselves, and how to speak appropriately. We have trained them for living, and have tried to form the character of Christ in them.

We expect more of them now than we did when they were babies. I think that is what God expects of us. The longer we walk in response to grace, the more like Jesus we ought to become. Every morning I pray, "God, do whatever is necessary in me and to me and through me that I might be more like Jesus tonight when I go to bed than I was when I got up this morning." Every day we are to be growing to be more and more like Jesus. When we follow the path of the good news from the holiness of God to the grace of Christ to holiness of life—that is when we really understand grace and that is what we are called to offer people.

Our message is grace in all of its fullness.

Our Model

We need to have a model for living a life in response to grace.
Sometimes we need to remember who we are and whom we belong to!

My life is nothing really spectacular. I come from pretty common stock. My grandparents on each side were ordinary folk. I am a living example that God does not call the qualified, but he qualifies the called. I carry something in my pocket to remind me of my roots. It is my grandpap's coal car check, a coin hung on the side of a two-ton car of coal which ensured that that particular miner would be paid for the coal he had dug. My mom's dad was Frank Hubbard. He was a coal miner. He had to go to work in the deep mines of southern West Virginia as a young boy after his father was killed. He worked for over fifty years by the sweat of his brow and the strength of his back digging coal—first by hand, then by machine. It was the ravages of that life that cut his life short.

He was an extraordinary man. He never completed the third grade, but had more wisdom and faith in his pinky than many of us can fit into an entire lifetime. He was a strong, yet humble man. He always took up the cause of the one who was less fortunate than he was. He was a leader whom people followed because of the way he treated them—not because of the positions he held. He died when I was about thirteen.

Several years ago, I was leading a Volunteer in Mission trip to southern West Virginia to work among the poor in McDowell County, where my mother grew up. While there, we visited the demonstration mine in Gary, West Virginia. My grandfather had worked as a foreman in that mine at one time. An older, retired miner was walking and talking us through the mine. His gait, build, and speech reminded me of my grandfather. I found myself lagging back from the rest of the group, trying to be quiet and remember what it was like to hear the sound of his voice and the depth of his wisdom.

At the close of the tour, the guide and I struck up a conversation. I told him that my grandfather had worked in this mine, and that this was an important part of my heritage. He asked my grandpap's name, and when I told him his name was Frank Hubbard, the man's face smiled with a knowing look of recognition. He told me that my grandpap had been his first boss in the mines. He shared words that made a grandson's heart pump with pride: honesty, integrity, and faithfulness. He shared that my grandpapa had rescued him from a mine explosion and had saved his life a few times because of his skill and knowledge. He then went and checked the records; he returned with this small coin as a reminder of my grandpap and the person of character that he was. I carry this to remind me that I come from humble beginnings, and that I should treat all people as persons of worth. Because ordinary people have extraordinary worth in God's eyes. But there is one who is a far greater model for the life of humble servant-leadership.

Our model is Jesus who, though he was God, did not count equality with God as something to be grasped. Jesus who emptied himself, taking on the form of a servant. Jesus who was born in human likeness and humbled himself and became obedient to the point of death, even death on a cross. Jesus who said that those who would come after him must deny themselves, take up their cross daily, and follow him. Jesus who modeled servant leadership embodied in love. Jesus who told those who follow him that those who would be great in his kingdom would be servants of the rest. Jesus who said that those who would be first would be last. Jesus who was no respecter of persons. Jesus who said whoever would save his life, will lose it, but whoever loses his life for my sake will find it. Jesus the embodiment of grace. Jesus the servant leader.

To lead is to serve. Servant leadership is what we are about. We hold that our model is Jesus, and we will strive to live each day in response to his grace, and model what that kind of leadership looks like. It is about Jesus, and living in response to his grace.

CHAPTER ONE

APOSTOLIC AND POSTMODERN CHRISTIANITY

Joel B. Green

R eferring to the French Revolution, Charles Dickens opened his book *A Tale of Two Cities* with those now-famous words, "It was the best of times, it was the worst of times." How one judges such things is often a matter of perspective: best for whom? Either way, knowing "the times" is the first challenge, and this is certainly the case for Christians engaged in mission in the early twenty-first century. Not unlike the heady days of the French Revolution, we are caught up in changing times, rapid in the pace of their transformation, seemingly cosmic in their reach. Ours is not an era without a compass, however, as though we were the first to occupy this particular frontier. In many ways, our present is a rehearsal of a bygone time, the period of earliest Christianity we sometimes call the apostolic age. This is the world of the first century, the time of Jesus' ascension, the coming of the Spirit at Pentecost, and the launching of the missionary church. How can looking backward in time give us direction for the future?

A number of questions come to mind. How is our world, the world of the early-twenty-first-century United States, like the apostolic era of the first century? What challenges do we share? What opportunities? Are we engaged in mission that is well suited to our context? These are important questions for those of us in the Wesleyan tradition, for whom identity and vocation find their focus in spreading scriptural holiness across the land.

Let me begin by sketching how we might compare the world of the ancient Roman Mediterranean and America at the turn of the twenty-first century. In doing so, I need to admit that I can paint this portrait with only the broadest of strokes. I can make only broad generalizations, overlooking any number of finer details. With this caveat, I want to suggest some parallels that are interesting, attractive, and thought-provoking as we place these two worlds side by side, our world and the world of Peter and Priscilla, Phoebe and Paul. I want to sketch four analogies, then propose for each a challenge and an opportunity for those of us who want to be the missional church today. After this, I want to make a few observations about the character of the church and its mission for people who understand the times in which we live.

The Presence of One Superpower

First, the *oikoumene*, or "civilized world," knows only one superpower. This is true for Roman times and for our own era: the world knows a single superpower whose interests and values are difficult to escape, whether one is living within its borders or beyond.

I use the term "civilized world" not simply because this is the way that Rome referred to itself. "Civilized world" is also useful in contemporary parlance for the way it speaks to our American fascination with putting our nation forward as having a superior and enviable way of life when compared to other countries. Of course, it is also true that there may have been other, lesser powers in the first century, as there are today. However, when one inhabits the margins of the civilized world, the presence of a superpower can still be felt. Its values have a way of pressing on the lives of everyone.

I vividly recall a conversation I shared with a colleague while copastoring a church in Berkeley, California—a bilingual, bicultural church, with overseas-born, Mandarin-speaking Chinese persons comprising roughly one-half of the congregation, and the other half made up of American-born, English-speaking Chinese and, in some cases, their Euro-American spouses. One of my primary responsibilities as pastor was to preach each week in English with my counterpart, Dr. Jun Choi, providing continuous translation. Our routine was to meet early in the week in order to discuss the biblical text and talk through the sermon, attending especially to issues of intercultural communication. How might the message be shaped and translated so as to take seriously the differences of cultural background among those gathered on Sunday morning? What did I need to learn this week about a culture that I was still trying to learn, that of our overseas-born Chinese congregants? On this particular occasion, I was working with Deuteronomy 34, noted the emphasis on Moses' age in this text, and wondered aloud what it would mean to speak of "growing old before God," given how age and the elderly were viewed among many Americans. I wondered what could be said in a context where those influenced most by mainstream American values worshiped the idea of youth, whereas those influenced most by traditional Chinese culture would take for granted that with age came esteem, that to be old would be to be highly honored. Dr. Choi, himself Shanghai-born, urged me forward, insisting, "No, no, we have been in America too long. Even though we may not have been born in America, we have started to act like you and live like you!" Even those on the margins can experience the overwhelming presence of the influence and values of the regnant superpower.

In the ancient world, one of the ways this took place was through the importance of religion, and especially through the worship of the emperor of Rome and the cult of the goddess of Rome, *Roma*. Not unlike the power of civil religion today, Rome had its own ways of broadcasting its importance throughout the world. This propaganda was typically communicated in terms that were strikingly religious. Caesar was "savior of the world," the epoch of empire was the "age of salvation," and the life record of the emperor could be called the gospel or "good news." Caesar owed his own rule to the beneficence of the gods. The glue of Rome and the Roman empire was worship—worship of the Roman emperor as at least son of god, if not as god; and of *Roma*, the goddess of Rome. Hence, to threaten or call into question the Roman Empire or Roman rule was to call into question or threaten the gods themselves. Religion was not one aspect of life easily cordoned off into its own sphere; religion was everywhere and everything was religious.

The parallels with our own culture are easy to draw. Witness, for example, the difficulty our own churches have of extricating the worship of Jesus as Lord from various forms of nationalism. Note how churches struggle with the uneasy presence in the primary place of worship each Sunday of two icons, the cross of Christ and the Stars and Stripes. What does it mean to have those symbols in the same house devoted to worship on Sunday morning? Witness the relationship between faith and politicians at least, if not faith and politics. In the 2004 elections this was inescapable, even if critical discourse about the relationship between faith and politics was less easy to locate. And witness the ease with which in our own country the call to support the government is morphed into a call to honor God. This all sounds very first-century Roman.

Under this broad heading of the *oikoumene*, we could also point to the reality of calculated national self-interest parading as beneficence. On the whole, superpowers are best known not as serving the hands of God, not for being the hands and feet of God in the world, nor for putting into play God's ways. Rather, superpowers are best known for the decisions they make in their own self-interest. Typically for nation-states, self-preservation is the highest, divinely authorized value, the end that justifies any and all means, but superpowers have a way of masking self-interest by encouraging others to view their actions as beneficent and for the good of the people. For example, Rome might and in fact did claim that bringing peace to other regions in the world exhibited its beneficence toward the world. The same might be said, and indeed was said, of Rome's making travel more safe or increasing production lines from one place to the other. All of these can appear to be actions for the sake of the people. In reality, however, these were acts of calculated self-interest. Rome did away with sea piracy in the Mediterranean in order to get grain from the fields of Egypt to warehouses in Rome. Travelers in parts of the Roman Empire today can walk on the remains of Roman roads, so well were they built, but we should not forget that road construction was motivated by the need to support the movement of the Roman army throughout the Empire.

If the portrait I am painting is true in broad outline, then what are the challenges that face people who live in such a world and seek to engage in mission as God's people? Among the possibilities, one of the more urgent is surely the challenge of maintaining a prophetic voice of witness. Too easily, the Christian voice is co-opted by the voice of empire. With one voice, the voice of empire speaking so clearly, so loudly, other voices can hardly rise above the din, and the voices of minorities are altogether lost. In such a world, Christian voices are easily lost and, what is worse, are easily co-opted. Our Christian language becomes their political language, so to speak. Public discourse is shaped by so powerful a force that alternative discourses are difficult to obtain.

One contemporary illustration of the situation we now face is the important thesis of Yale law professor Steven Carter. In his book *The Culture of Disbelief*, Carter observes how important it is in America today to be religious.[1] In the United States, however, both political and legal systems compel believers to subordinate their personal religious views to a public faith largely devoid of religion. For the Christian community, this means that, while I might be encouraged to exercise my beliefs in the privacy of my inner life or home, powerful forces press me to hang my religious commitments at the door prior to leaving my house each morning. More broadly, we have learned to compartmentalize sacred from secular, and thus to imagine that some aspects of life, such as the gathering of God's people for worship or the solitude of prayer, are permeated with holiness in a way not available in or appropriate to our workaday lives.

From the early days of Israel's nationhood, prophets provided an alternative voice, speaking on God's behalf, giving God's perspective on contemporary realities. The power of the monarch was held in check by the authority of prophetic voices. In the book of Acts, the Spirit fell on God's people for the clear purpose of generating a prophetic community (Acts 2). What happens when the voice of empire is the public voice, the voice of faith a private one? In an important sense, this is a form of taming or even silencing the voice of Christian communities.

What of the opportunities in such a world for mission-minded people? A lot depends on how we locate ourselves in this world. In his study *Jews in the Mediterranean Diaspora,* John Barclay introduces some helpful language for grappling with the experience of "not living at home," that is, of living in exile.[2] *Assimilation,* he writes, is a measurement of social integration, including social interaction and practices. *Acculturation* refers to the degree of a group's linguistic, educational, and ideological achievement within an alien culture. Finally, *accommodation* draws attention to the practical utility of acculturation, whether to embrace or resist one's surrounding culture. These are helpful distinctions because they suggest something of the continuum along which an exiled people might relate to the dominant culture within which they find themselves. We might learn a new language, and so appear to be assimilating fully into an alien culture, only to use that language in the service of resistance. Or we might learn a new language, which we use when we must to exchange goods in the marketplace, but privately nurture our ancestral language—

and with it, our ancestral identity. In fact, the Jewish experience of dispersion is marked by stories both of acceptance and resistance, sometimes heroic. The same can be said of the lives of Christians in exile, Christians living in a foreign land, not at home. We are often led to think that the only options before us are to be like everyone else or to withdraw from the world, but Barclay's categories help us recognize a wider array of possibilities for authentic faith and witness.

"When in Rome, do as the Romans." Getting along in the world is easily equated with such slogans. It is better not to create unrest or to draw dreaded negative attention upon oneself or one's community, we might be told. I find it hard to imagine how we who look to the Scriptures for meaning and divine direction, these Scriptures in which the death of Jesus Christ figures so prominently—the death of Jesus by crucifixion at the hands of the Romans—could adopt such a perspective on life in the world.

How to respond? The options before us are basically the same options available to Christians in the first century. Among these are two that early Christians in ancient Rome declined: violent resistance to the superpower and retreat or withdrawal, revolutionaries on the one hand and sectarians on the other hand. There is a third option, and it is the one most present in the Gospels and Acts, or 1 Peter and Revelation. This is the option of critical, faithful engagement. This is the option John embraced, and which led to his exile on Patmos (Rev 1:9). Were we to practice the work of a prophetic community, a community known for staying in there and engaging with critical witness, we too might find ourselves exercising prophetic ministry outside the halls of political and social power.

The Economics of Daily Life

Returning to my portrait of parallels in the world of ancient Rome and the world in which we make our homes, let me draw attention, second, to the economics of daily life. Of course, our economies, Rome's and

America's, are vastly different, but similarities are noticeable. For example, both the Roman world and our own have experienced increased urbanization. We can easily document the huge chasm segregating the haves and the have-nots. We can note the ongoing polarity between country and city folk, country and city life.

Consider Paul's treatment of the common meal among the Corinthians, for example, in 1 Corinthians 11:17-34. Here, Paul deals with what happens when the Corinthians gather for a supper whose character, he says, is to have been determined by the Lord. In sketching the divisions at Corinth, he actually employs the language of the haves and have-nots: "What! Do you not have homes to eat and drink in? Or do you show contempt for the church of God and humiliate those who have nothing?" (1 Cor 11:22). As Paul clarifies in this text, this socioeconomic problem is theological, but this is only a reminder that sociology and economics never exist outside the purview of theology. Money *is* a God matter.

Let me mention another example from the larger Roman world. Cities and towns did not develop big governments. Indeed, the treasury of each was purposely kept small in order for the urban wealthy to give money for projects like building aqueducts or public buildings. This was so that the honor for the gift could come back to the giver. We know these kinds of things because we have seen plaques that read, "in honor of ___." These were money and gifts given in order to draw attention to the goodness of a person or family, often with strings attached. Giving is often a public event so that the giver is able to gain the recognition, honor, and even political support of the larger public. And this is a very Roman way of thinking.

To think like ancient Rome on these matters is to contemplate the close relationship between power and wealth. What are the challenges that come with this way of looking at reality? Remember that humorous twist on the Golden Rule: Whoever has the gold, makes the rules! And this raises the question, *When is adopting the economics of this world an implicit agreement to embrace for oneself the sign of the beast (see Rev 13)?*

When is participation in a particular economic enterprise tantamount to the participation in the economy of 666?

What is the opportunity for folks who live in such a "civilized world"? Luke envisions faithful response in terms of a community marked by hospitality and open-handed *koinonia*. In Acts 2:42-45 and 4:32-35, Luke uses language like "the believers held all things in common" or "from time to time, whoever had sold and gave, and it was given to those who had need" (author's translation). Here "fellowship" (or *koinonia*) is amplified, especially in economic terms. This does not mean that fellowship is simply to be *identified* with economic sharing, but rather that economic sharing is a characteristic and concrete manifestation of the unity of the believers. Those who were baptized are now "those who believe," and their common faith is manifest materially in economic solidarity. The picture Luke paints does not focus on the ideal of poverty nor on the evil of material possessions nor even on total renunciation as a prerequisite for discipleship. Selling what one has is customary within the community Luke depicts, but such giving is voluntary and is oriented toward addressing the plight of the needy. In Acts 2, Luke demonstrates that the pentecostal outpouring of the Spirit signifies nothing less than the long-awaited restoration of God's people.[3] And the gift of the Spirit has as its immediate consequence certain defining practices of the community, including economic sharing.[4]

Thinking back on the Gospel of Luke, we can see how Luke prepared us for this emphasis through Jesus' teaching on and practices regarding money and meals. From his inaugural address in Luke 4:16-30 to the meal on his last evening with his disciples (Luke 22:24-27), Jesus worked to show how table fellowship and economic sharing without regard to issues of status were expressions of the gospel of the kingdom of God. "Good news to the poor" is correlated with "the year of the Lord's favor" in Jesus' reading of Isaiah's promise of Israel's restoration (Luke 4:18-19), and this is now manifest concretely in the life of the community of believers. It is no surprise, then, that, in Acts 4:32-35, Luke characterizes community practices with language from Deuteronomy 15: "there was not a needy person among them." This was to have been a qualification of God's people delivered from Egypt in the exodus, and it is now the qualification of God's people restored in new exodus.

Similarly, in Acts 16, the Philippian jailer and his family take Paul and his company in their home and take care of their wounds and feed them, extending hospitality to them. This is nothing other than being open to God and responding to God's grace, an open-handedness toward God that compels one likewise to adopt a posture of open-handedness to those in need. To be open to God is to be open to those in need; one cannot clutch tightly to what one has and be open to God.

Religion, Religion Everywhere

The third major point of comparison between these two worlds, ours and that of Roman antiquity, is related to the first, but it deserves more specific attention: Religion, religion everywhere. In the age of the Enlightenment we learned antagonism to things spiritual. Whatever else it does, the term *postmodern*, now widely used but little understood, suggests that we have moved beyond the Enlightenment. The result is that, today, we reflect more and more the common life of Rome. This is a world of gods and temples, with day-to-day existence lived out in the presence of and under the influence of spiritual powers. In this world, the gods are many and tolerance is a celebrated virtue. Is this not the world in which we now live, or are at least moving toward?

I was fascinated to read in our local newspaper, the *Lexington Herald-Leader*, that the magazine *Seventeen* now devotes a column to religion and spirituality. Teenage debates on religion can now be found in the pages of a magazine better known for articles about how to match lipstick to blush, not for exploring the concept of a higher power. But under its editor-in-chief, the venerable girls' magazine has added a faith section that includes inspirational messages, personal stories of spiritual struggle, and testimonials on issues including prayer and more. What is more, we were told, the content is serious. Verses from the New Testament are printed alongside sayings of the prophet Mohammed; teachings of Pope John Paul II are featured side by side with the teachings of the Dalai Lama. This is a fascinating representation of life in the empire, since here is firsthand evidence that taking religion seriously means opening the cafeteria to all kinds of possibilities. Here is a virtual cornucopia of spiritual possibilities. Interestingly, journalist Rachel Zoll reported in her story that people are tired of the feel-good, nebulous spirituality of the baby boomers, are now looking for something concrete, and are finding it in various kinds of religions.[5]

What kinds of issues does that raise? On the one hand, antiquity can be characterized as an expression of polytheistic syncretism, a kind of vegetable soup of religion. Here are all sorts of gods, a little here, a little there, a good representation of what we may find in the modern-day new-age movement. This portrait contrasts sharply with the biblical focus on one God, monotheism, and especially on the one God who is known to us in Christ, christocentrism. Basically, the problem confronting us in the New Testament is this claim that Jesus is the definitive expression of God's character and purpose. That is, in a world accustomed to many gods and many paths to salvation, Scripture presents the God of Israel as the one true and living God, the God of Abraham, Isaac, and Jacob; this is the God who raised Jesus from the dead, the God revealed to the world definitively in his son, Jesus of Nazareth, Lord and Christ. Jesus is not one Lord among many; "he is Lord of all" (Acts 10:36).

Among the questions we face today is a closely related one, how to talk about salvation in a world where salvation is not needed—or, better, a world where the paths to salvation are many: salvation as education and salvation as therapy, for example. How does one even begin to raise the question of the pervasive human need of a savior? This is the problem of a world becoming more and more like the Roman world of antiquity.

Lurking in the shadows of this portrait of the world is the reality of the status of Christianity as a minority movement, a tiny group within the great expanse of the Empire. I am often asked, *Why did those Christians not do something about the Roman Empire?* But what would a handful of followers of a crucified Messiah do about Rome, a city of a million persons?

I was reared in West Texas, where the presence of the church was strong and politically important. Folks wanting to run for public office would note on their campaign brochures and political advertisements that they both attended the downtown church and taught Sunday school. Living for a number of years first in the northeast of Scotland and then the West Coast of the United States presented me with a different reality. Practicing Christians were not so numerous; their political weight was negligible. Followers of Christ were at best simply one group among many, suggesting the importance of spirituality and, at worst, were implicated in all of the excesses of Christendom historically, from the Crusades on.

Religion, religion everywhere: the challenge here is that, when pluralism is the default public position, then tolerance is the most important value to be served. But this is not only a challenge but also an opportunity. When religion reenters our public life, then new possibilities are available for a church bent toward mission. In Acts 13, we find that Paul can go to the synagogue in Antioch and, based on Israel's Scriptures, based on their common understanding of faith before God, he can quickly sketch the grand story of Israel. And the narrative he relates follows a story line that reaches its culmination in Jesus, as though God's sending forth a savior, Jesus, was nothing but the most natural and perfectly logical outcome of God's plan. On the other hand, turning the page to Acts 14 or 17, we find Paul in an altogether different context, in the Gentile worlds of Lystra or Athens. Somehow, building on the religious sensibilities of these people, he is able to bring the good news of God's work to bring salvation. No less than in the Jewish world of the synagogue in Antioch, he finds evidence of God's work in the changing seasons and in a Gentile altar to an unknown god. Pointing to this evidence, he presents God's character, God's purpose, God's mission. In a world that others might find to be overwhelmingly godless, Paul sees a great place to do evangelism.

Our churches often flee from such possibilities, pulling in the welcome mat against a world that seems to be set against the call to love God and love one's neighbor. Is this because we have not learned how to stay critically and faithfully engaged? Have we not often failed to take seriously our own theological tradition, which presses us to find evidence all around us of the grace of God at work? Is it not true that heightened interest in religion is itself evidence that God is drawing attention to God's self, even if it is also true that many people do not recognize which god is beckoning to them, calling their names?

Life in a Melting Pot World

The last point of similarity between the Roman world and our own is this fantasy that we live in a melting pot where all the peoples of our worlds are basically like us. One of the inescapable features of empire is cultural diversity. This is because persons from previously well-boundaried lands begin to mingle, trade, and intermarry. In the Roman world, this was helped along by new trade routes, a remarkable system of roads, the open sea, and more. In the contemporary world in which we find our homes, this mingling of different peoples is nothing but faster and more advanced, due to stunning advances in technology, in transportation, the communication industry, and so on. Empire forces a common language— in the world of Rome, Greek; in the early twenty-first century, English, and American English at that. Classes are offered in order to teach American accents. Even China has mandated the learning of English in schools. The language of air travel, the language of science, and, increasingly, the language of theology is English.

If we speak the same, are we not the same?

In reality, the world in which many of us live today is very much like that experienced by Christians in Roman antiquity, but perhaps not in the way one might expect. Although a certain level of tolerance was expected and practiced in the ancient Mediterranean world, this tolerance had its limits and, in particular locales, one finds significant restraints on acceptable socioreligious behavior. This is true in our own world. Much more pressing, however, is the reality that, within the Roman Empire, one finds an all-pervasive understanding of the way the world works, which was by definition a religious narrative that shaped life in all of its dimensions. The ethics of patronage that characterized relationships of all kinds in the Roman world underscored the importance of status and located all persons—irrespective of religious commitments or purity or family heritage or ethnicity—within a web of obligation that had as its focal point acts of reverence to the gods and goddesses to whom the emperor and, thus, the empire owed its success.

In such a world, acceptance within one's community and status within one's social world were grounded in conformity to accepted norms, living according to the rules of the household over which Caesar was head. Everyone had a place, and everyone acted according to his or her place— this was the glue of the empire. The pluralism of Rome could be stretched only so far before those who did the stretching found themselves outside the community, residing in a state of ostracism, suffering, and shame, boycotted from normal social intercourse. If "glory" or "honor" (*dōxa*) were the fundamental social currency of the Roman world, what of Christian communities? Would they not appear to have experienced bankruptcy, socially speaking?

Both the pluralism of the Roman world and that of our own world are false. There are deep-seated stories that inform our lives and that provide the grid by which we read and shape how we embody the faith of our ancestors. Pluralism assumes cohabitation of diverse commitments, but in our world we find world-shaping stories that are so totalizing that they throw up walls against the biblical narrative. For those who inhabited the New Testament world, those guiding narratives had to do with Roman conquest and the ethics of obligation and status; the household of Caesar depended on these formative stories. We have our own versions, our own life-forming, grand narratives, such as:

- "The little engine that could"—if only it worked hard enough and kept pushing and kept pushing, it could conquer that mountain.
- The promise of "unrelenting progress"—a kind of social and religious and political Darwinianism that has long been integral to the nation's self-consciousness, and which is expressed in the church through one of our hymns: "For darkness shall turn to dawning, and the dawning to noonday bright; and Christ's great kingdom shall come on earth, the kingdom of love and light."[6]
- "I did it my way" or "Be all that you can be" or "We give you what you want when you want it"—a portrait of life expressed in search for selfhood that, almost invariably, leads to radical individuation, as if to say that maturation comes as we learn "to give birth to ourselves."

Biblical visions of the church and of Christian faithfulness are often wedded to that other vision, the American dream: Anyone can be a winner! Find the right formula! You can rule the world! I can determine my own destiny! And so around coffee tables at denominational meetings, for example, church leaders can be heard beaming with news of growing churches, larger buildings, and more expansive budgets, while others stare at the ground, embarrassed at their failures. After all, measures of faithfulness more congruent with faithfulness to Yahweh are hard to place into statistical tables in an annual report. These measurements of success, as Leviticus 19 has it, would include family and community respect (vv. 3, 32), religious loyalty (vv. 3b, 4-8, 12, 26-31), economic relationships (vv. 9-10), workers' rights (v. 13), social compassion (v. 14), judicial integrity (v. 15), neighborly attitudes and conduct (vv. 11, 16-18), distinctiveness (v. 19), sexual integrity (vv. 20-22,

29), exclusion of the idolatrous and occult (vv. 4, 26-31), racial equality (vv. 33-34), and commercial honesty (vv. 35-36).

In such a context, the fundamental question is, *Whose guiding narrative, whose grand story do we embody?* Is it the ethics of obligation and status? Is it "the little engine that could"? Is it a millennial vision that promises either doom and gloom before the end or a kind of Darwinian evolution of the church? Or is it the narrative of God's engagement with Israel as we have learned to read it through the life and message of Jesus of Nazareth?

What Sort of Mission?

Given these contemporary echoes of the world of ancient Rome, what is our mission? How might we think about the mission of the church? In the first century, Luke the Evangelist concerned himself with this question. What might we learn, were we to take seriously the missional message of the Gospel of Luke and the Acts of the Apostles (that is, Luke–Acts)? Let me outline two considerations.

On the Frontiers of Mission

Participating in a pastors' training event among Nazarenes in Northern California, I was struck by the opening word of encouragement the superintendent gave to those gathered. Forget about those special parking places by the church office door and make no plans for climbing the ecclesial ladder, he told them. Ministry in Northern California, he observed, was not about status or career or marks of professionalism. "We don't have a district office," he said. "We have a mission center." Bivocational ministry and bilingualism would be the order of the day for ministry in the new millennium, he predicted. The message was clear: folks called to minister in Northern California in the 1990s and beyond would have to set aside the tried-and-true ways of doing church. On the frontiers of mission, Christian leadership must let go of "what worked over there" in favor of renewed commitments to the leadership of the Spirit, discernment, creativity, and vision. As Peter put it, drawing on the words of the prophet Joel, the new age inaugurated by the outpouring of the Holy Spirit would be the time for dreaming dreams and seeing visions (Acts 2:17).

If this is true for Northern California in the 1990s, it was certainly true of the Roman Empire in the mid-first century. It is increasingly true of ministry throughout the United States.

As we read the pages of the New Testament book of Acts, we do not see Paul, Peter, and Stephen perusing the shelves of the local bookstore to find out how to grow a church, to discover seven ways to start a successful small group. There were neither such bookstores nor such books. Folks who live on the frontiers of Christian mission search in vain for how-to manuals. Those books have not been written. No one has been there before. There are no tried-and-true techniques for those who are truly living on the frontiers of mission.

This does not mean that we are without resources, however. There is the long narrative of God's engagement with God's people. And we recognize from that narrative, and from Acts even more pointedly, that there is no missional frontier where God has not already prepared the way. We are not taking God where God has not gone before, though we may be going where the church has never gone before—or where the church has long ago lost its foothold. When there are no tried-and-true techniques, one is pushed back onto other kinds of foundations, onto foundations other than the way someone else did it in some other place. The church in Acts finds its orientation for the mission above all in the Scriptures of Israel as these are interpreted by Jesus and in light of his ministry, death, and exaltation—and in prayer. Let me develop these two points in a little more detail.

The Scripture-Scape of Mission

The extraordinary mission of the church in Acts does not mark the departure of the church from the long history of God's engagement with Israel. The "new thing" of the church's mission is not unprecedented. Rather, we find the followers of Jesus reading the story of God in the Old Testament through fresh eyes. They see themes and commitments in the Scriptures of Israel that others had largely overlooked or forgotten. They reread the Scriptures of Israel in ways that directed them to extend the good news to people heretofore and otherwise on the margins or beyond the boundaries of God's people.

On the face of it, the Scriptures forbid access to the temple on the part of the Ethiopian eunuch (Acts 8:26-40), for example. In spite of his devotion to God, he was still a eunuch, so he could never be admitted to "the assembly of the LORD" (Deut 23:1). Luke sketches the encounter between this eunuch and the evangelist Philip, however, as an intimate exercise in scriptural interpretation, a small Bible study held on an oxcart.

> Philip ran up . . . and heard him reading the prophet Isaiah. He asked, "Do you understand what you are reading?" He replied, "How can I, unless someone guides me?" And he invited Philip to get in and sit beside him. (Acts 8:30-31)

Philip reads the words of Isaiah as a reference to Jesus. In doing so, however, he finds that the marginal status of the eunuch is addressed, and overturned, in the story of Jesus' death and resurrection. Just as God had raised Jesus up from the dead, so God would reverse the status of this eunuch, in continuity with God's own promises:

> Do not let the eunuch say, "I am just a dry tree."
> For thus says the LORD:
> To the eunuchs who keep my sabbaths,
>   who choose the things that please me
>   and hold fast my covenant,
> I will give, in my house and within my walls,
>   a monument and a name

better than sons and daughters;
I will give them an everlasting name
that shall not be cut off. (Isa 56:3b-5)

And so, having heard the good news, the eunuch requests and receives Christian baptism, then goes on his way rejoicing in his salvation (Acts 8:35-39).

In the same way, it is through interpretation of the Scriptures that Peter proclaims the exaltation of Jesus as the inauguration of the new age of the Spirit, when the Spirit would be poured out on all people (2:14-41). It is through interpretation of the Scriptures that Paul receives the authority to take the good news not only to the Jews but also the Gentiles (13:45-49). And it is through interpretation of the Scriptures that the church determines that Gentiles are embraced within the people of God without their first having to be circumcised (15:13-21).

According to Luke, the church learns the inexorable relation of Scripture and missionary mandate in the life and teaching of Jesus. When setting out his identity and purpose, Jesus had turned to the Scriptures, citing Isaiah 61:1-2: "The spirit of the Lord GOD is upon me!" He had interpreted his vocation in terms of the Scriptures, showing how "good news to the poor" (Luke 4:18-19) is worked out in relation to the least and the lost: widows, Gentiles, lepers, and the like (Luke 4:21-30).

We who find ourselves living on the frontiers of Christian mission are not left simply to our own devices. The church finds its orientation for the mission especially in the Scriptures of Israel as these are interpreted by Jesus and in light of his ministry, death, and exaltation.

Prayer and the Mission

Throughout Acts, prayer provides the opportunity for the disclosure of God's purpose, not least at pivotal points in the progress of the church's mission. Of course, God communicates his will in a variety of ways in

Acts—angelic visitation, interpretation of Scripture, and the intervention of the Holy Spirit, and so on, but among these prayer figures prominently.

Consider, for example, the conversion of Cornelius and his household, and Peter's subsequent sharing of table fellowship with these new believers (Acts 10:1–11:18). Mission among the Gentiles and sharing hospitality between Gentile and Jew constituted a theological and missional departure of such enormity that it was important to demonstrate that this innovation bore the divine imprimatur. In fact, Luke's story virtually brims with confirmation of the divine hand at work, seen not only in the intervention of divine messengers, but especially in the strategic role prayer has to play. Cornelius, though a Gentile, is a man of prayer (10:2); on a certain day, he has a vision at three o'clock, which Luke has already associated with a time for prayer in the temple (3:1). That the vision takes place in the context of prayer is suggested by the angel's words to Cornelius, "Your prayers . . . have ascended as a memorial before God" (10:4), and confirmed in Cornelius' report to Peter of this episode in 10:30-31. What occurs with Cornelius is paralleled by the experience of Peter, who likewise has a vision while praying (10:9), and later has opportunity to speak of his prayer and vision (11:5). In both cases, the will of God is revealed—both with regard to these individuals who are praying and, more significantly, with regard to the makeup of the people of God. At stake in this instance is not the legitimation of the communication of the gospel to Gentiles; this, after all, has already been mandated by the risen Lord (1:8) and performed by Philip (8:26-40). Instead, full and open hospitality was at stake (note the protests against such interchange by Peter himself in 10:28, then by some in Jerusalem in 11:2-3). In this case, then, prayer is the means by which God's will for full fellowship between Jewish and Gentile believers is revealed and enacted.

Similarly, Paul's own call to bring the good news to the Gentiles is associated with prayer (9:10-16; 22:17-21). While in worship and fasting the church in Antioch experiences the Holy Spirit as God's mission-sending agent, and the church sends Paul and Barnabas out in prayer and blessing (13:1-3). And so on.

This does not mean that the purpose of God is somehow set loose in prayer. Such episodes as these reveal rather that God is already at work redemptively. The question is whether people will recognize and, having recognized, embrace and serve God's purpose. In Acts, prayer is a means by which God's aim is disclosed and discerned, and prayer is the means by which people get in sync with and participate in what God is doing.

Embodying the Gospel

Acts presses the question whether the church has gotten the gospel right. Again and again we find in the book of Acts the struggle that takes seriously the message as this was articulated and put into practice by Jesus in the Gospel of Luke: "The Spirit of the Lord is upon me / . . . to bring good news to the poor" (Luke 4:18). Notice especially those points in the narrative where Luke uses the phrase "the word of God grew." This phrase appears in Acts 6:7; 12:24; 19:20, each time marking the cessation of opposition, signaling the advance of the missionary movement in the midst of persecution, and anticipating the next major development in the narrative. Taking this emphasis on the progress of the word seriously capitalizes on Luke's thematic development of the "word of salvation" (13:26, author's translation) as well as the effects of the word—that is, its germinal role in the production and growth of the people of God (see Luke 8:4-15). Typically, this phrase comes after the church struggles with the nature and outworking of its own message, with getting the gospel right, with grasping and embodying fully the message of Jesus, with putting the word of God into play.

This imperative to get the gospel right comes first in our understanding that it is not about us. It is about God. It is realizing that God has more at stake in the integrity and truth of the gospel. It is God who seeks us out. Thus, for example, the prayer Luke records in Acts 4:23-32 is not about the church's need for rescue. This may be surprising, since Peter and John, and with them the whole church, have fallen into trouble with the Jerusalem leadership. Rather than simply lift up their troubles to God, however, the church draws God's attention to his own agenda, aims, and purpose. Addressing God, the church asks that God might act in ways consistent with his own aims and promise. It is about God, what God can do to make sure that his agenda is accomplished.

In part, getting the gospel right is an issue of *content*, sketched repeatedly in the mission preaching of Jesus' followers and agents of mission. This content has a narrative shape, following the plotline leading from God's redemptive actions and promises of old to the actualization of those promises in the advent of Jesus Christ, whose death and exaltation enable and call for human responses of faith and repentance, symbolized in baptism; and to the consummation of God's purpose in "times of refreshing" and "universal restoration" (Acts 3:20-21). Additionally, getting the gospel right has to do with the *performance* of the good news in the lives and through the missional outreach of the community of the baptized. The narrative of God's actions continues, exhibited in the lives of God's people. Embodying the gospel in acts of worship and practices of hospitality (2:42-47) and broadcasting the gospel in places of teaching and worship and day-to-day business—these are nonnegotiable demonstrations of the authentic gospel.

The Church and Its Mission

As Christian Scripture, Acts bears on how we think about and practice Christian faithfulness. The immediacy of Acts for today's church is highlighted all the more by the significant points of contact between the world of Acts and our own. Though ancient Rome and the United States today are not identical, we have seen remarkable parallels, and these press us to recognize anew the character of a minority church in a vast empire, empowered for and charged with missionary witness.

We might say to ourselves, *We need first to get our act together as a church. Let us first clean up our own backyard. Let us first get to the place where we embody the gospel and then we can carry the gospel to others.* For Luke, this is a deeply troubling and erroneous way of thinking. For Acts, the church will never "find itself" except insofar as it does so in mission. The church will never embody the gospel apart from engagement in mission. To put it more strongly, the church does not "do" mission, but is itself defined in mission. This is because mission is at the heart and built into the DNA of the church. The church cannot embody the gospel among its own members and then engage in mission since the church cannot be the church apart from mission, just as the gospel cannot be the gospel apart from mission. In short, for the church that would find its mandate here in Acts, there is no escaping the missional nature of the church.

THE CHURCH AND CHANGE: WHAT CAN WE LEARN FROM OTHER HISTORIC TRANSITIONS?

Meesaeng Lee Choi

W
hat are the four major eras of Christian history? What might we call each era? What role did the church of Jesus Christ play in each? How did context impact the life, structure, mission, and ministry of the church in each era? What were the roles of clergy? Laity? Denominational systems? How has theological education led or followed each era of change? In light of the grand sweep of church history, what challenges face us as we seek to be faithful to our Wesleyan-Methodist tradition concerning the mission of the church?

What are the four major eras of Christian history? The question itself is challenging. At the dawn of this third millennium, still one-third of the world population of six billion comprise unreached people groups.[1] Four eras of Christian history? This is a luxurious question. Since William Carey launched the modern missionary movement (1792), Christians in many parts of the world where the gospel has been preached have been facing struggles from each era—early, medieval, and modern—or some mixture of them all at the same time, within their short Christian history.

However, as the Cuban native, American-educated historian Justo L. González rightly points out, globalization in church history should be discussed from two different perspectives: geographical and chronological. "If geographical globalization seeks to open new horizons by taking students to Central America or to East Africa, chronological globalization seeks a similar end by taking them to the fourth or to the tenth century."[2] From this perspective, then, to speak of "historic eras in flux" is a worthwhile endeavor. I will divide the history of the church into four eras: the Early (to 313 C.E.), the Medieval (313–1521), the Modern (1521–1960s), and the Postmodern (1960s–present). In order to anticipate our interest in the nature of the church's presence and mission in the world, I will refer to these eras as the Apostolic Era ("Early"), the Age of Christendom ("Medieval"), the Evangelical Era ("Modern"), and the New Apostolic Age ("Postmodern").

The Apostolic Era (to 313 C.E.)

For the first three centuries, the church was an illegal, oppressed, and persecuted minority within the Greco-Roman world and in every foreign land. Its focus was on outward witness. The good news of Jesus Christ for the whole of humanity moved east across Asia as early as it moved west into Europe, moving beyond a number of political, cultural, geographical, and linguistic borders.[3] Christianity took hold first in Asia. Indeed, according to Samuel Moffett, Asian Christianity mounted global ventures in missionary expansion that the West would not match until after the thirteenth century.[4]

Compelled by the risen Lord, the disciples reached beyond the boundaries of Israel to bring the message of God's universal reign through

Christ initially into cities, and later into the surrounding countryside. Along with the honor of the suffering Lord and the urgent expectation of the return of the Risen Lord (or *parousia*), persecution and martyrdom played an enormous role in shaping Christian self-understanding and the nature of the church.

During the spread of the apostolic movement, the first followers of Jesus were committed to writing several missionary texts known as Gospels, which called for a radical act of conversion. People from widely diverse social and cultural locations joined the world Christian movement. While confronting misunderstandings of its own message, competing worldviews, and accusations (e.g., by Celsus and Porphyry), the church defended its faith through apologetic writings.

As the church grew, there was unity across the empire on the major points of Christian doctrine. The church referred to itself as "catholic" and all who deviated from this common, universal faith were labeled "parties" or "heretics." The early church faced growing challenges from such heretics as the gnostics and Marcion, who created their own systems of doctrine. Three major developments in response to heresies and major consequences for the future church were: apostolic succession, the rule of faith (eventually formulated as the Apostles' Creed), and canonization of the Scriptures of the church. Each in its own way helped define the church.[5]

The Christian community, or local church, functioned as an education center to train leaders by transmitting the teaching of the apostles, and followed the model of the school of Gamaliel, the teacher of Paul (see 2 Tim 2:2). Attempts to fuse pagan and Christian learning were developed by theologians such as Clement of Alexandria (c. 150–c. 217) and Origen (c. 185–c. 254) in Egypt, and later Basil the Great (c. 330–379), Gregory of Nazianzus (c. 330–390), and Gregory of Nyssa (c. 330–c. 395) in Asia Minor. The aim of Christian education was to produce a learned and cultured person (in the liberal arts), who combined knowledge of Scripture with pagan thought.[6]

Around 200, the Christian clergy emerged as a specialized priesthood of sacramental, holy orders (in which the power of Christ's presence resided), removing church leadership from ordinary life and displacing the New Testament emphasis on gift and *charisma*. Leadership became increasingly hierarchical with the development of a single bishop (*mon-episcopacy*), in contrast to the pluralistic ministry of apostles, prophets, evangelists, pastors, and teachers (Eph 4:11; cf. the *Didache*).

The Age of Christendom (313–1521)

The year 313—when the church became an official religion of the Roman Empire with the Edict of Milan, which allowed religious freedom for Christianity[7]—marks the beginning of Christendom.[8] The image of the church as a minority band (the persecuted church) following in the footsteps of an alternative Lord from the margins of society disappeared. In its place stood the imperial church, with an exponentially increasing number of congregations accommodating themselves to the ruling system. Despite the fact that emperors called the ecumenical councils and their decisions fluctuated with the position of the emperors, the tradition of the church became a theological problem in its own right as the church sought to determine which councils were authentic and authoritative.[9]

Membership in the church through the initiation of baptism was concomitant with citizenship in the state. The focus was on power structures (i.e., *caesaropapism*—the authority of the Western papacy over the Eastern, ecumenical patriarch), dogmas, institutionalization, and denominations (i.e., the Great Schism between the Western Roman Catholic Church and the Eastern Orthodox Church in 1054).

However, when the multitude entered the church, monastic reactions provided a radical alternative. Based on Christian principles— which found common ground in prayer, shared property, and mutual support—monks and nuns renounced imperial society (a physical separation from the inhabited land) and established an alternative society (heavenly realities on earth).

The church became a static people focused on worship, sacrament, and spiritual care, with a settled and pastoral leadership. The apostolic and evangelistic/missional nature of the church evaporated. The emergence of celibacy among the clergy accelerated the division between church leadership and laity.

Throughout the medieval period, the papacy and the episcopacy became more and more a means of personal aggrandizement (with bids for these positions marked by violence, simony, *nicolaism*, and lay investiture).[10] Those who yearned for reform took the monastic life, leading to a series of renewal movements through the Cluniacs (tenth century), the Cistercians (twelfth century), and the Mendicants and the Beguines (thirteenth century). Papal reform (*reformatio*) repeatedly (and, in many cases, vainly) attempted change by abolishing simony and by promoting clerical celibacy (eventually made mandatory in 1079), but not the monastic ideal of poverty. The Great Reform movement in the papacy was essentially a reordering of the fabric of the medieval church and its institutions according to a model of papal monarchy. The papal reforming effort in this period was fundamentally moral, not so much theological or spiritual. The movement culminated in the Fourth Lateran Council in 1215, which is known as Innocent III's great reforming council (the last one until the next, the Council of Trent in 1545–1563, which was held during the Counter-Reformation).[11]

During the Era of Christendom, Christian monasteries functioned as theological education centers—copying, preserving, and studying the Scriptures and other theological writings. Priests and pastors were trained, and candidates for the offices of bishop and pope were nurtured.[12] During the Carolingian revival of learning (*Renovatio*), schools were developed. Out of the reforming monastic orders, the local episcopal schools, and the cathedral schools, the medieval universities (e.g., Paris, Oxford, and Cambridge) grew and scholastic theology flourished (note the synthesis of faith and reason by Thomas Aquinas, the epitome of high scholasticism).[13]

Both Western Latin Roman Catholic and Eastern Greek Orthodox Christians were challenged and surrounded by the spread of the Islamic movement and the Islamic conquest (622–1453). During this era, Christianity in Africa survived the advance of Islam in Egypt (where the Coptic churches survived as long-term minorities), Nubia, and Ethiopia (where the church took the form of isolated majorities), but not further west.[14] Catholics in Moorish Spain were the resistant churches, and the churches of Asia (e.g., the Nestorians in Central Asia and China) became extinct. By the tenth century, the Christian expansion across central Asia to China occurred mainly through the work of East Syrian (Persian) monks and nuns, priests, and merchants. Monasteries functioned as centers of worship and evangelism, inns for Christian merchants, centers of medical care, schools, and as settings for Syriac texts (Scripture, liturgy, and the stories of saints and martyrs) to be copied and translated.

In the Age of Unrest, also known as the "Age of Reform,"[15] different ways of seeking reform arose, including the conciliar movement and late medieval mysticism. One followed the path of institutional renewal, while the other sought reformation through a deeper spiritual life oriented toward an immediate and personal relationship with God. A third mode of seeking reform was through direct, local acts of practical, doctrinal, and structural reformation, including the work of such persons as John Wycliffe, John Hus, and Savonarola.

The Evangelical Era (1521–1960s)

With the recovery of apostolic preaching, the Protestant Reformation provided new definitions of the true church based on the marks of pure doctrine (the word of God preached) and pure sacramental administration (baptism and Eucharist, with both bread and the cup).[16] Additionally, the church of Christendom was fragmented. The Protestant movement challenged and reformed the inherited priestly categories of leadership in the direction of a more pedagogical identity for the clergy; the clerical paradigm remained, however.

The churches of the Reformation were to provide an educated clergy as well as to instruct the community of believers. The regular preaching of such reformers as Ulrich Zwingli in Zurich and John Calvin in Geneva provided "a prime example of this drive to instruct the laity in the truth of the Christian religion."[17]

The following generations of the reformers elaborated theological details with ever-increasing specificity. This degenerated into a Protestant scholastic orthodoxy that, like its Catholic counterpart, was sterile, devoid of spiritual vitality, and of little interest to any but academics. Religious wars continued and denominational divisions proliferated (e.g., Lutheran, Reformed, Anabaptist, Anglican, Congregationalist, Baptist, and Presbyterian). A number of motivations for the fracturing of the church could be named, but doctrinal beliefs in relation to the teaching of Scripture were central. Key issues included the doctrines of salvation (soteriology); the church and its worship, sacraments, and leadership (ecclesiology); and the authority of the Bible over church, pope, and tradition.[18]

From the mid-seventeenth century (the time of René Descartes's death) through most of the twentieth century, Western culture developed under the influence of Enlightenment thinking, in which reason was given priority over all that was conceptual, doctrinal, and dogmatic. Key features of the Enlightenment were "autonomous individualism, narcissistic hedonism, and naturalistic reductionism."[19] This was the age of skepticism, historical dissolution, and flight from traditional authority. As James McClendon and Nancey Murphy claim, in modernism, epistemology became the center of philosophy, replacing cosmology and metaphysics.[20] The Enlightenment exercised great influence on a global scale. The mission of the American churches became a channel for modern Enlightenment-oriented higher education to other areas of the world. Along with this, the doctrinal views of particular denominations were taught in pulpits throughout the world by home and foreign missionary programs.

However, from a more global Christian and especially Protestant perspective, the modern era can also be viewed as "evangelical."[21] As a young Roman Catholic, Martin Luther discovered *iustitia Dei*—a spirituality grounded in justification by faith—and the theology of the cross, and the Protestant (*evangelisch* in German) movement broke from the Roman Catholic Church in the sixteenth century. Despite the subsequent hair-splitting doctrine debates within Lutheranism and religious wars, the rise of Pietism out of Protestant scholastic orthodoxy nurtured a more organic understanding of salvation—"new birth" or "regeneration" in the place of a forensic understanding of imputed justification—in the seventeenth century. The rise of the evangelical Christianity of John and Charles Wesley out of Anglicanism renewed Christian faith in England and influenced American Christianity with a religion of the heart and sanctification (scriptural holiness) in the eighteenth century.[22] In America, the Great Awakenings and the repeated resurgence of revivals in the eighteenth and nineteenth centuries, and the Methodist and Holiness movements with their slogan of "Scriptural holiness throughout the land" in the nineteenth century, led to the rise of the Pentecostal movement, with a theology and experience more focused on the Holy Spirit, in the twentieth century.

Beginning from William Carey's modern missionary movement (1792), then Hudson Taylor's Faith Mission movement, the Protestant foreign mission had become transdenominational, interdenominational, and ecumenical, culminating in the First World Missionary Conference, which was held in Edinburgh in 1910.

The New Apostolic Age (1960s–Present): New Christendom?

The fourth era of Christian history, the postmodern era, grew out of modern rational conflicts, which led to radical relativism and pluralism. Generally speaking, postmodernism knows no absolute truth, emphasizing instead a subjective agreement within a community. Postmodernism is often characterized by its emphasis on chaos (or complexity), uncertainty, otherness, openness, multiplicity, and change. According to one metaphor, postmodern surfaces are not landscapes but "wavescapes," with the waters always changing and the surface, lacking any boundaries, never the same.[23]

When considering Christianity in the emergence of the new global reality in this twenty-first century, we can view Christian history from a fresh perspective.[24] It is as if we are seeing Christianity again for the first time (radical discontinuity). The challenge is to see Christianity not just for what it is, but for what it was in its origins (historical continuity) and what it is going to be in the future (New Apostolic and New Christendom).

A New Christendom

The postmodern era can be viewed as a "New Christendom." One of the main reasons for this is a demographic shift. Over the last 500 years, the majority of Christians lived within the sphere of European, Christian civilizations. However, the center of gravity in the Christian world has shifted inexorably to the south: to Africa, Asia, and Latin America. This is "southern Christianity," according to Philip Jenkins.[25]

This is a *New* Christendom since it is not just a transplanted version of the (old) medieval Christendom. Old Christendom offered a common culture and thought-world, but also widespread intolerance symbolized in aggressive crusades, heresy hunts, and religious pogroms. This is a New

Christendom. To borrow Benedict Anderson's phrase, here nation-states are imagined communities of relatively recent date, rather than eternal or inevitable realities.[26]

Some view the New Christendom as a Christian subculture, not a governmental entity but an "economic entity."[27] Members of "southern Christianity" are likely from among the poor, often unimaginably impoverished by Western standards.[28] They acknowledge biblical notions of the supernatural, such as dreams and prophecy, exorcism and healing, and give serious attention to persecution and martyrdom as relevant apostolic themes for their situation, especially in places like Guatemala, Rwanda, and Sudan. The social and cultural impact of Christianity in "southern Christianity" is inconceivable for Americans and Europeans.

Alister E. McGrath believes that the new fault lines will feature Christianity and Islam.[29] Many, including Jenkins, predict that there will be inevitable Christian-Muslim conflict.[30]

A New Apostolic Era

Ecclesiologically, we can describe the postmodern era as "New Apostolic." According to the *World Christian Encyclopedia*, independent or postdenominational Christians are the second largest bloc in the world after Roman Catholics (more than 20 percent among 2 billion Christians as of 2000).[31] Most outnumber all Protestants, Orthodox, and Anglicans, and they are called postdenominational since most exist outside the structures of historic, traditional, denominational Christianity. They comprise the only Christian bloc growing faster than the global population and faster than Islam. They are the fastest growing major religious movement of any kind in the world today.

This era is "New Apostolic" because the focus of these congregations is on apostolic and evangelistic missions (as in the New Testament church), thus breaking with more traditional notions of church. "Southern Christianity" is founded and led by a loosely structured apostolic network of leaders (mirroring a recovery of the apostles and prophets). And these congregations have spearheaded church planting in ways reminiscent of the first century. (Recall that John Wesley did evangelistic, apostolic ministry outside the structures of, and without the blessing of, the denominations of his day.)

The New Apostolic paradigm involves a "change in attitude, from one of institutional maintenance [within traditional denominational structures] to one of incarnational mission and power in the Holy Spirit."[32] Here, local churches are directly involved in spreading the gospel in other lands. Outreach is considered to be just part of the DNA of the church.

It is interesting that, in the fifth century, *vita apostolica* ("apostolic life"—that is, living in the manner of Christ's closest followers, the apostles) was understood as life in a religious community (see Acts 2:41-47; 4:32-35), but in the twelfth century the description of the disciples "sent out" began to gain favor (see Luke 9:1-6). Apostolic life was characterized primarily by poverty of life, itinerant preaching, and by involvement in the world rather than flight from it.[33] The Mendicants and Beguines were the climax of these spiritual ideals of Christendom.

The call in the church today is for apostolic leadership. Emerging apostolic leaders are visionary, missional, empowering, team-oriented, and reproducing. They are Bible-centered and kingdom-conscious rather than oriented toward institutional maintenance.[34]

Conclusion

We should recognize the rise of postdenominationalism as a change or transition rather than as the death of denominations. From 1960 to 2000, membership in mainline churches decreased 21 percent, from 29 million to 22 million.[35] However, as Cecil Sherman predicted, "Denominations are going to stay alive."[36] We will continue to have Roman Catholicism,

Eastern Orthodoxy, and Protestant mainline churches in "historic eras in flux." In recent decades, various renewal organizations formed within these denominations, calling for reform. Their goal is neither schism nor takeover, but to mobilize God's people in mission, polity, discipline, theological education, worship, and discipleship. Thomas Oden discusses the relationship between gospel and church in these terms:

> It is this gospel that created the church. The gospel does not belong to the church, for the gospel brought the church into being (Eph 5:23; Col 1:18-24 . . .). The church that forgets the gospel of salvation is finally not the church but its shadow. The church that becomes focused upon maintaining itself instead of the gospel becomes a dead branch of a living vine. The church is imperiled when it becomes intoxicated with the spirit of its particular age, committed more to serve the gods of that age than the God of all ages.[37]

Indeed, recall that Wesley did not worry over the continuing existence of Methodism. "I am not afraid that the people called Methodists should ever cease to exist either in Europe or America. But I am afraid, lest they should only exist as a dead sect, having the form of religion without the power. And this undoubtedly will be the case, unless they hold fast both the doctrine, spirit, and discipline with which they first set out."[38]

As we understand our own historical era more clearly, we see the need to continue to be involved in God's renewing and reforming work in the church. Our perspective must be global, encompassing, catholic, and holistic, and more importantly, it must be one of "marginalized incarnation,"[39] with our lives oriented, like that of Jesus, toward the margins rather than the center, the cross rather than the crown.

CHAPTER THREE

GRACE IN A POSTMODERN WORLD

Steve Harper

W hen Rick Warren wrote the first sentence of *The Purpose Driven Life*, I doubt that he had any sense that he was authoring one of the best-selling non-fiction books in the history of publishing. And when that first sentence read, "It's not about you," I also doubt that he realized he was opening the door for the message of grace in a postmodern world. When "it's not about you," it must be about someone else—and that is the starting point for the message of grace.

This should be very good news for those of us in the Wesleyan tradition, because we understand the heart of the gospel to be a theology of grace: prevenient, converting (justification and regeneration), sanctifying, and glorifying. Each dimension of grace points to the fact that God has taken initiative in Christ to save us and to do so when we were powerless to save ourselves.[1] This begins with the earliest moments of our lives, and it continues all the way to the time of our death. A theology of grace—as an order of salvation—provides us with the concept for declaring to the world, "It's not about you." We are not in search of a message; our challenge is how to present this message in a post-modern world.

I believe that postmodernism is real, that it is here to stay, and that we have no choice but to proclaim the gospel in the context of it.[2] Although I will not attempt to set forth everything that might be said about post-modernism, it is helpful to sketch some of the generally accepted tenets of it, recognizing that there has been (and continues to be) disagreement as to what postmodernism specifically includes.[3] Nevertheless, there is a consensus on the following elements:

- postmodernism rejects the existence of a single, universal worldview.
- postmodernism rejects a focus on rationality.
- postmodernism rejects the idea of inevitable progress.
- postmodernism rejects the view of "human conquest."
- postmodernism rejects the notion of universal truth.

It is not enough simply to recognize what is being dismissed in a post-modern world; we must also know what is being embraced. The following elements summarize that side of the matter:

- postmodernism emphasizes holism (affection, intuition, and cognition).
- postmodernism emphasizes life in the larger ecosystem.
- postmodernism emphasizes life in community.
- postmodernism emphasizes "truth for the community."
- postmodernism emphasizes diversity.

This results in what we might call a cultural dynamism, or a phenome-non that cannot be ignored in the world today, nor in our proclamation of the gospel in this world. We can trace postmodernity as a movement:

- from industry to information
- from local to global
- from unity to diversity
- from mass production to targeted preferences
- from a center to multiple centers

My exposure to historical theology leads me to believe that ours is by no means the first generation to see the emergence of the elements I have just cited. This removes the edge from any radical separation between "then" and "now." It is not correct, in my judgment, to make the last forty years of the twentieth century appear to be categorically different from any age previous to it. At the same time, I agree with scholars of postmodernity when they posit that the convergence of so many of these elements in such a short span of time does create a new worldview, and all the more so when the technological revolution is included in the picture.

Shortly before his death years ago, I heard Francis Schaeffer identify a fundamental mistake among Christians, and especially Christian leaders: trying to live in the world as it used to be, or in the world as they wish it were. Schaeffer declared forcefully that the only option we have is to live in the world as it is. In a similar way, this is where I stand in relation to the need to take postmodernism seriously and to address the world as it is with the gospel.

Against the backdrop of these very brief summaries regarding the dimensions of grace in Wesleyan theology and major dimensions of a postmodern ethos, I want to focus on what I am calling "the contours of grace"—that is, the attitudes and actions required of us Christians if the gospel of grace is to be heard and received. I do not mean to disparage the importance of content, but rather at this moment to emphasize that the message of grace must be communicated in both substance and spirit, so that others can experience grace and grow in it. What might this look like?

First, we must realize that moving into a postmodern world has neither changed nor diminished people's need for grace, nor their desire for it. A week's worth of viewing Oprah, Wayne Dwyer, and Dr. Phil confirms the pain and lostness of people today. All our advances and alterations have not enabled us to save ourselves, and the God-shaped vacuum is still in the human heart. As Christian communicators, this means we will recognize that the need to offer grace is as great as ever, and our commitment to do so cannot be less today than in any period of history. Indeed, that Rick Warren can sell more than 20 million books to people who are willing to seriously entertain the notion that "it's not about you" is an indicator that people today are still hungry for grace.

I believe this need for grace is occurring particularly in the context of recovery from brokenness, woundedness, and abuse. We have an open door into the lives of millions of people for whom feelings of shame, rejection, loneliness, and fear are everyday experiences. But how we walk through that door can make all the difference. The message of grace declares that Jesus understands our suffering because he suffered, and he invites us to take our pains to him without fear of condemnation.[4]

Second, we must realize that untold numbers of people no longer associate grace with Christianity; even fewer associate grace with the church. In his book *What's So Amazing about Grace?* Philip Yancey recounts a friend's experience with a prostitute in Chicago. The woman came to him in desperation over her own life and the life she was now forcing her two-year-old daughter to have in the sex industry. The friend asked if she had ever thought about going to a church for help. The woman exclaimed, "Church! Why would I ever go there? I was already feeling terrible about myself. They'd just make me feel worse."[5]

Those of us who have lived and worked in a "church culture" most of our lives can barely imagine how widespread this view is in the world today. The very people Jesus spent time with and attracted to himself were often the ones who would not see him today or respond to his message. And they fail to do so primarily because the church has so caricatured Christ that people turn away from him, rather than toward him—without ever realizing that what they are actually doing is turning away from us, not from Jesus.

We are the ones who have made Christ and the Christian life appear cold, judgmental, and legalistic. We are the ones who have made the gospel appear to be something that can be affirmed in words, but denied in deeds. We are the ones who have made church appear to be a place where people who have it "all together" can gather and look down on those who do not. We are the ones who have created a gospel of "un-grace," so it should come as no surprise when people do not see grace in the church.

If we are to communicate the message of grace in a postmodern world, we will do so in terms and in places that do not carry the weight of such caricatures. And this is something that Wesleyans should understand. For in the eighteenth century, the Church of England (and other churches as well) were failing to reach the masses. The early Methodist movement not only saw this sad fact, but also organized itself to target the "forgotten people," whom God had never forgotten in the first place.

Third, we must realize that the message of grace will necessarily be communicated more by laity than by clergy. If people do not see grace in the church (either because they are not there, or because they do not experience it when they come), they must see it in the society. And that is where 99.9 percent of the people of God are located every day. Getting the message of grace into a postmodern world will require a deep recovery of the priesthood of all believers. The clergy filter is clogged; the laity pipeline is our best hope. To accomplish this, however, will require a massive recovery of the vision that all Christians are ministers.[6] It will demand an ethic of holiness and a commitment to holy living in the marketplace. To a great degree, every church will be a "seminary"—a seed plot where disciples are helped to see their role as grace dispensers, and are then trained to engage in that ministry each day where they live and work.

Viewing this from the Wesleyan tradition, it means equipping the laity to use the order of salvation to assess their environments and to determine the best way for communicating grace in them. Such a view would operate something like this:

- **Prevenient Grace:** Who are the people in my relationships who appear to be aware of their need for grace?
- **Converting Grace:** Who are the people I know who are at the place where they can hear an invitation to attach themselves to grace through an initial commitment to God in Christ?
- **Sanctifying Grace:** Who are the people in my fellowship who are ready to advance in the life of grace and become deeper disciples of Christ?
- **Glorifying Grace:** Who are the people I know who are living near the end of their time on the earth and need assurance that they are God's beloved children?

To be sure, this schematic hardly scratches the surface. There are many other items that attach to this view and many subcategories to be developed. Furthermore, no single believer will be expected or trained to function equally well in every area. But this realization does mean that laity will be encouraged to look at life through the lens of grace and to consider prayerfully how to relate to others in a grace-filled way.

Fourth, we must realize that this approach means people will often (perhaps usually) experience grace before they are able to name it or understand it. A postmodern culture is one oriented around experience, and here is yet another place where the Wesleyan tradition should feel very much at home in communicating the gospel. We should be those Christians who know that the fruit of the Spirit (Gal 5:22-23) is the primary bridge over which the message of grace travels. We should be those who understand that many will taste grace before they can define it.

This will mean that the traditional evangelical paradigm of "believe, then belong" will have to be reversed as people "belong, then believe." This change of strategy will not frighten Wesleyan believers, however, because we already know that this is precisely how the Wesleys designed early Methodism to operate.[7] We will remember that most conversions in Methodism took place *after* men and women had been accepted into the Societies and Classes—*after* they had been exposed to the gospel and to true believers for a while. Because it was Christian experience that creatively blended "tell me" and "show me," the converts to Christianity in the early Methodist movement were well positioned for growth in grace and "going on to perfection."

In some ways, the early Methodists were ahead of their time in recognizing that the profound assimilation of an idea takes time, and it occurs best in an environment where hospitality, honest inquiry, and perceived relevance are experienced by the seeker.[8]

They understood the value of cultivating genuine Christian experience in the context of sustained Christian conference. Recognizing this, we will refrain from caricaturing experiential Christianity as touchy-feely, and we will instead seize the opportunity to "offer them Christ" in the context of supportive community. We will believe that God wants people to know God more than we want them to know God, and that the doorway of experience is one of the ways we have of facilitating that today.

Finally, we must realize that offering grace in a postmodern world will be what it has always been—costly. We will not sell "Christianity Lite." We will not separate knowledge from vital piety. We will not settle for an affective outcome that leaves people superficially entertained. We will communicate sound doctrine and challenge people to embrace it with all their heart, soul, mind, and strength.

We will not minimize the cross or the timeless need for all of us to repent and believe the gospel. We will not be content to have members, but will press forward to make disciples. We will not allow people to descend into privatized spirituality, but will continually call them into Christian community and servant life in the world.

Likewise, we will not settle for "Christianity Same." Rooting ourselves in Scripture, we will nevertheless recognize the need to exegete our multicultural world to discern the paradigms, narratives, and languages that best communicate grace in particular contexts. We will not fall prey to the notion that there is a sacred code language that must be used with all people in all situations. We will prayerfully ask God to make us creative messengers who can enter our respective contexts with the gospel of grace. Eugene Peterson's question for pastors can become a guide as we ask, "Who are these particular people, and how can I be with them in such a way that they can become what God is making them?"[9]

Finally, we will move into the world fully aware that even our offer of grace will be misunderstood, and sometimes rejected—both by unchurched and churched people. In this regard, I believe it will take more grace on our part to offer grace to others in a culture that so easily distorts it—sometimes in very gross ways. We will have to put on the whole armor of God before offering grace in a postmodern world—but that has always been so. We will have to make sacrifices we did not have to make when a Christendom model prevailed, when civil religion propped up the church, and when "churchianity" was good enough. We will be called to "turn the other cheek" and "endure to the end" as we incarnate grace, communicate it, and invite others to receive it. In our postmodern world, Bonhoeffer's aversion to "cheap grace" will still be required.

But as we realize these things (and many other things that will surface on this journey), we will also know what preceding generations of grace offerers have known—that, best of all is, God is with us! We are not alone. The Lord of the Harvest will not only send us into the fields. He will see to it that we do not return empty-handed.

HOLINESS OF HEART AND LIFE IN A POSTMODERN WORLD

Howard A. Snyder

I s the message of holiness still relevant in a so-called postmodern age? Or in a *post*-postmodern age? I believe it is. Paradoxically however, the relevance of the holiness message for today becomes clearest when we first go *back* and reexamine what the Bible says about the holiness message, examining it again in light of the questions and challenges of today.

The church has always been the most prophetic when it has rediscovered the relevance of the "eternal gospel" (Rev 14:6) for a new age. My thesis is that the biblical message of holiness is pointedly and powerfully relevant to the world in which we live. But to understand God's call to and provision for holiness, we must see it within the context of the *whole* call of God. What does it really mean, biblically, to speak of the whole gospel for the whole world? Too often we pull apart things that should be held together. The need for biblical comprehensiveness is especially important when it comes to the subject of holiness. Holiness *should* mean wholeness, the integrity of heart and life. Therefore we should pay close attention to the *full scope* of God's call upon our lives, upon the church. This we will attempt to do. We want to see, for instance, how the call to salvation, the call to ministry, and the call to holiness all fit together as one story, making one picture.

I am structuring this essay around what I am calling *the five calls of God.* We will examine what the Bible says about God's intent for humanity and for God's creation. We are called to holiness. But that call is part of a larger intention of God to bring salvation in its fullness. We need to understand the *call to* holiness, and the *grace of* holiness, in the context of the full biblical witness of God's intention for people, cultures, and in fact the whole creation.

We will examine these five calls of God more or less in the order in which they appear in the Bible—that is, in a history-of-redemption sequence. There is a story here. We can trace it through Scripture, and even up to today and into the future—postmodern or not. God is up to something, and God graciously calls us to be part of this great work. We are a called people. The final goal is "a new heaven and a new earth," the time when the kingdoms of this world "become the kingdom of our Lord and of his Messiah" (Rev 11:15); when "every knee [shall] bend, / in heaven and on earth and under the earth, / and every tongue . . . confess that Jesus Christ is Lord, / to the glory of God the Father" (Phil 2:10-11).

If we are to play the role God intends in this great drama, we must be a holy people. In fact, God calls and *invites* us to share his nature and his holiness, for his own good pleasure and purposes. What then are these *five calls of God?* And what do they have to do with holiness?

The Call to Earth Stewardship

We begin with the first one we find in Scripture: *the call to earth stewardship.* This may at first seem a strange place to begin, but you will soon catch the drift of the story.

We read in Genesis 2:15, "The LORD God took the man and put him in the garden of Eden to till it and keep it." The NIV renders the commission as to "work . . . and take care of" the garden. This is a commission to all humankind, of course, not just to males. In the Genesis account "the woman" has not yet been created, but the joint commission is clear in 1:28: "God blessed them, and God said to them, 'Be fruitful and multiply, and fill the earth and subdue it; and have dominion over the fish of the sea and over the birds of the air and over every living thing that moves upon the earth.'"

"Dominion" here clearly refers to stewardship or nurturing management, not selfish exploitation. John Wesley understood this very well. He wrote of this passage, "Man, as soon as he was made, had the whole visible creation before him, both to contemplate, and to take the comfort of." Made in God's image, man and woman have "the government of the inferior creatures" and are "as it were God's representative[s] on earth."[1] This is why Wesley says in his sermon "The Good Steward": "The relation which [humankind] bears to God . . . is exhibited under various representations," including that of sinner. "But no character more exactly agrees with the present state of man than that of a *steward*. . . . This appellation is exactly expressive of his situation in the present world, specifying the kind of servant he is to God, and what kind of service his divine master expects of him."[2]

Affirming man and woman as stewards of God's good gifts, including the created order, is thus basic biblical teaching and has been fundamental in Christian history and theology. The call to earth stewardship predates the fall. It is an early commission given to all humankind—therefore, today, to all nations, peoples, and governments, and not just to Christians. But sound biblical exegesis, viewing the combined callings of God, bids Christians in particular to be committed to protecting and nurturing the physical environment. As Sandra Richter eloquently points out, the sense of Genesis 2:15 is that the Lord God put the human in the garden to serve and guard it. She writes that "the larger message" of the creation accounts is clear:

The garden *belongs* to Yahweh, but [humankind] was given the privilege to rule and the responsibility to care for this garden under the sovereignty of their divine lord. This was the ideal plan—a world in which [humankind] would succeed in constructing the human civilization by directing and harnessing the amazing resources of the planet under the wise direction of their Creator. Here there would always be enough, progress would not necessitate pollution, expansion would not demand extinction.[3]

Earth stewardship can properly be called *creation care*.[4] It is the faithful human nurture and management of the God-created order. For Christians, creation care is an integral part of the faithful following of Jesus Christ and the worship of the Holy Trinity.

This then is the first of the five calls of God. We may view earth stewardship or creation care as the broadest circle of God's call. It is a call to all humanity. All men and women were and are called to care for God's good earth, thus fulfilling their mandate to be God's regents on earth. We are to serve and honor God by caring for his creatures; to worship and glorify God by our work and our enjoyment of the garden God planted. To understand God's call to holiness, then, we need first to understand the *context* within which that call comes: The call to earth stewardship. But this in turn leads us to the second call of God.

The Call to Covenant Peoplehood: Repentance, Faith, Obedience, Community

The second biblical call we must consider is *the call to covenant peoplehood*. This call appears in Scripture after the fall. It is the beginning act in God's initiative to restore and heal a fallen creation. It is foreshadowed by the call of Noah to build the ark,[5] but the call to peoplehood really begins with the call of Abraham and Sarah in Genesis. It continues through Isaac and Jacob and then expands as Israel becomes a nation.

We know well the Genesis and Exodus stories. God liberates Israel from slavery in Egypt and forms a covenant people for himself. He gives his people not only his law—itself a revelation of God's character—but a whole way of life, an identity and a future as God's special people.

The Bible is explicit that this call was for God's glory and for the sake of all peoples and nations. The call is the expansion, partial fulfillment, and development of God's word to Abraham: "In you all the families of the earth shall be blessed" (Gen 12:3; cf. 18:18; 28:14; Ps 72:17). Since humankind went astray, rebelled, and wandered from God, Yahweh raised up his own people, a holy people called to serve him both in worship and in witness. In the Old Testament this witness was largely in the form of a contrast society among the nations—his "peculiar people" and "priestly kingdom" (Exod 19:6 NRSV; Deut 14:2, 26:18 KJV; Titus 2:14 KJV; 1 Pet 2:9 KJV). But the Hebrew Scriptures also signal a broader, expanding, "centrifugal" mission to the nations. This of course is the background of Jesus' Great Commission in the New Testament to "be my witnesses in Jerusalem, in all Judea and Samaria, and to the ends of the earth" (Acts 1:8); to make disciples of all nations and peoples.

Notice especially the two main elements of this call: *covenant* and *peoplehood*. The first, peoplehood, reminds us that this call is not just to individuals. Rather it is a call to form, be, and act like a people—a human community in solidarity internally and with God. The second, covenant, reminds us that this call is not simply to be just *any* kind of people; simply one more people group among the nations and ethnicities of the earth. The point is to be a people in covenant with God—so closely connected with Yahweh that their actual way of life is shaped more by God's character than by the nations and cultures all around. God's people are to be salt and light—so faithful in their love relationship with God and in their revelation of his character that they season, heal, and illuminate the world rather than taking on the world's flavors or being dazzled by the klieg lights of the world and its enticing show.

In Scripture, the call to covenant peoplehood is unmistakably a call to holiness. This call to holiness for God's covenant people is explicit and emphatic.

Notice also that the call to covenant peoplehood is a call to *repentance, faith, obedience,* and *community.* Because of sin, we cannot simply of our own initiative become God's people. Here we face the biblical teaching about human rebellion and waywardness—the deep stain of sin that requires the healing medicine of salvation through Jesus Christ. The call is to be the redeemed people of God, the community of the Spirit, in the world. I do not need to elaborate these truths here, but we need to be clear about them. The call to covenant peoplehood is a call to transformation and healing—to turn from evil and alien ways to truly be the people of God *on the basis* of the provision God has made available through Jesus Christ.

The call to peoplehood is thus the call to salvation—to accept the healing offer of salvation that God graciously makes in Jesus Christ by the Spirit. This is a call God now makes to everyone, everywhere. God "now . . . commands all people everywhere to repent" (Acts 17:30); to repent and believe the good news (Mark 1:15). It is the gospel call to all nations, tribes, languages, and peoples. In this gospel age of the Spirit, especially, this means that those who are called become also those who call others. God commissions his called people to be his coworkers in the calling of the nations to Christ.

In terms of the five calls of God I am outlining here, we may view covenant peoplehood as a second circle inside the larger circle of the call to earth stewardship. The creation-care call is a call to all humanity, as previously noted. We see in Scripture, especially in the New Testament, that this "peculiar" call to covenant peoplehood ultimately *also* extends to all humanity. In the Bible the peoplehood call proceeds progressively from the call to Abraham and Sarah, to the whole people of Israel, to the ever-expanding body of Christ, and thus to all peoples everywhere. So we represent this second call of God as the circle of covenant peoplehood within the initial circle of earth stewardship.

The Call to God's Reign: Allegiance and Loyalty

Jesus said, "Very truly I tell you, no one can see the kingdom of God without being born again" (John 3:3 TNIV). But not everyone who is born again sees the kingdom of God! For many born-again Christians, the call to covenant peoplehood *exhausts* the meaning of God's call to humanity. Many people who have been converted to Jesus and the church have not yet been converted to Christ's kingdom. That requires a deeper, more comprehensive conversion. Much of the church thinks it is called only to be the church—that is, to be a community or organization that says, "Jesus Christ is our Savior," and that is it. The result is a sort of religious club, or a lifelong waiting room for heaven.[6] This is sad, for it misses another essential divine call. If you tend to think this way, I have news for you! Listen to what Jesus says. "Seek first the kingdom of God and his righteousness" (Matt 6:33 ESV). Pray every day, "Your kingdom come, your will be done, on earth as it is in heaven" (Matt 6:10 ESV). John Wesley comments that we should pray:

> May Thy kingdom of grace come quickly, and swallow up all the kingdoms of the earth! May all [humankind], receiving Thee, O Christ, for their King, truly believing in Thy name, be filled with righteousness and peace and joy, with holiness and happiness, till they are removed hence into Thy Kingdom of glory, to reign with Thee for ever and ever.[7]

This, then, is the call to the kingdom of God—the call to God's reign. It is a fundamental, biblical call. Scripture is all about God's reign, even where the precise term "kingdom of God" is not used. The Bible is a book about God's sovereign providential oversight, beneficent government, loving care and sure purposes, and concern with righteousness and justice. The kingdom call therefore concerns *allegiance* and *loyalty*. God's call upon us Christians is not just a call to repentance and faith; it is also the call to an allegiance above all other allegiances and a loyalty that trumps all other loyalties. It is a call not only to be God's church but also to serve his kingdom.[8]

At one level "kingdom of God" is really a metaphor reflecting a particular cultural context. Most nations today do not have kings, so the concept "kingdom of God" may for us lack concreteness. But the truth of the kingdom of God is not confined to cultural context, or to nations that have actual kings or queens. Faithful biblical exegesis concerning God's reign shows that a whole web of scriptural themes and metaphors weave together to teach us what the kingdom of God really means. These themes all make essentially the same point: God is "high over all," the one to whom we owe total obedience and loyalty. Yet he is a God of love whose rule and care are life-giving and beneficent.

More than a God who demands, the Holy Trinity is the Lord who *promises* the kingdom of God in its fullness. He is the *shalom*-promising God, the one with healing medicine for our bodies and souls, our land and all earth's cultures. The Bible makes the same point through various metaphors and word pictures—for example, the eloquent statement in Colossians 1:20 that through Jesus Christ "God was pleased to reconcile to himself all things, whether on earth or in heaven, by making peace through the blood of his cross." If we are well grounded in the Old Testament, we will not read the New Testament references to *peace* without thinking of the rich Old Testament meaning of *shalom*. The kingdom of God is the reign of *shalom* because of the nature and character of the Triune God.

The kingdom call is a call to kingdom values and virtues, kingdom ethics—to *really live* in the world so that we become *sunergoi*, "coworkers," toward the visible manifestation of God's reign on the earth.[9] It is a call for the church to *live out* the meaning of God's reign within our particular sociocultural contexts. It is a call to kingdom loyalty and allegiance—pledging allegiance first and above all to Jesus Christ and his purposes, thus viewing all other identities and allegiances as secondary. Our allegiance is to the Triune God and therefore to intentional solidarity with his people, our sisters and brothers in Christ throughout the earth. As a Jesus follower, my highest allegiance is not to my nation or party or president or state or social or ethnic group, but to Jesus Christ and the righteousness and justice of his reign.

So God's kingdom loyalty trumps national loyalty. The kingdom of God thus redefines, for example, the meaning of "homeland security." It calls us to the primary task of discerning the difference between kingdom allegiance and a proper national patriotism—a high-priority task for American evangelicals today, as well as for Christians in other lands.[10]

Jesus was explicit that the kingdom call is a call to the justice and righteousness of God's reign. The kingdom thus calls us to social and economic justice—to righteousness and justice in family and neighborhood, in and among the nations and families of the earth.[11] It is a call particularly to the poor and oppressed of the earth, for Jesus himself said, "The Spirit of the Lord is upon me, / because he has anointed me to bring good news to the poor" (Luke 4:18-19).[12]

In terms of the five calls of God, we picture this kingdom call as a third circle within the larger circles of earth stewardship and covenant peoplehood. It is not, however, a lesser or more restricted call. Rather, it is all that is intended to—and in fact *will*—penetrate to the farthest circumference, accomplishing God's overall, underlying, penetrating, constant purpose: That in all things, all places, all spheres, God may be glorified, his creation gladly serving and praising him.

This also is a call ultimately to the whole human race. But it proceeds through covenant peoplehood. That is, while people and nations and cultures everywhere are under God's sovereign government, it is God's special people, the church, who are called to be the initial visible embodiment of the kingdom of God—the community of the king.[13] The church is called to be God's subversive agency in the earth, constantly working—much of the time below the radar screen of the media—to witness to and actually speed the coming of the kingdom of God in its fullness.

So we may picture this call of God, this kingdom call, as a third circle within the calls to covenant peoplehood and earth stewardship.

The Call to Specific Ministry: Gifts and Particular Vocations

The Bible speaks of another very important call of God: *the call to specific ministry*. This is the fourth call of God we must consider.

The church has often discussed this call in terms of "vocation," or of "being called into the ministry." But how are we to properly understand this call biblically? How does it relate to the call to holiness? Are only "ministers" called to minister, or to live a high standard of holiness?

In the Old Testament we read of God calling Moses, David, Deborah, Esther, and Jonah, for example. These were all called to fairly specific ministries. They received calls unique to their lives and contexts. Paul said numerous times that he also was "called to be an apostle" (e.g., Rom 1:1; 1 Cor 1:1). Jesus called twelve apostles, but clearly these were not the only persons he called into ministry. He called many disciples, though relatively few apostles. Many men and women, many slaves and some masters, many poor and some rich responded. By the help of the Holy Spirit and the discipling process of the Christian community, these Jesus followers were able to discern and live out God's particular call on their lives.

Behind the reality of the New Testament church is an amazing, and socially unsettling, teaching of Scripture: *Everyone called to salvation is called also to minister*. Every man and woman, boy and girl whom Jesus calls to be a disciple he calls as well to be his ministering servant. There are no exceptions—no distinctions on the basis of wealth, class, gender, intelligence, physical characteristics, or ethnic or national identity. This is revolutionary! And the choice is up to the sovereign Spirit, not to us.

If we are rightly to understand the gospel and the call to holiness, we must also understand the call to particular ministry. The Bible gives us a rich and fully practicable theology of the ministry of the whole people of God. We need to mine it, understand it, and apply it in all our churches. *This is absolutely essential* if the church is to be the agent of God's reign as Jesus intends, and to be his holy covenant people.

Unfortunately, most of the literature on ministry that has accumulated over the centuries assumes that the subject of *ministry* concerns only *the ordained ministry*. This is grossly misleading. It is not possible to understand biblically the meaning of the church's ordained ministry if we do not see this more specialized ministry within the context of the *universal* call to ministry—the call God graciously extends to every believer to be a minister and servant (*diakonos*) of the good news.

Scripture reveals a clear and rich doctrine of the ministry of the whole people of God. This teaching rests on three pillars. All three have Old Testament roots and are elaborated in the New Testament as essential aspects of the New Covenant in Jesus and the new age of the Spirit. Here are the three pillars:

First, the priesthood of believers (1 Pet 2:4-10): Old Testament Israel was called to be a kingdom of priests, God's priestly people among the nations. Within this general call was the more restricted Levitical priesthood. This Old Testament history lies behind the New Testament teaching.

We learn in the New Testament, particularly in Acts and Hebrews, that the new covenant brings two key changes to the Old Testament priesthood. First, the priesthood is narrowed to just one person: Jesus Christ, our great High Priest, through whom we have salvation and receive the call to discipleship. But second, the priesthood is *expanded* to include all believers—fulfilling the original intention of a faithful, holy, priestly people in the earth. To be a Christian is to be a priest of God.

This is just what Israel's prophets foretold. Peter announced on the day of Pentecost,

This is what was spoken through the prophet Joel:
"In the last days it will be, God declares,
that I will pour out my Spirit upon all flesh,
    and your sons and your daughters shall prophesy,
and your young men shall see visions,
    and your old men shall dream dreams.
Even upon my slaves, both men and women,
    in those days I will pour out my Spirit;
        and they shall prophesy." (Acts 2:16-18)

In other words, all Christians now live in the pentecostal dispensation when the Holy Spirit has been poured out on all believers—precisely so that we can be God's witnesses, King Jesus' priestly people in the earth.

Second, Jesus' high priestly work and the pouring out of the Spirit open the door to another foundational pillar: the gifts of the Spirit. Just as every Christian is a disciple, so every believer receives special gifts for ministry. No one is left behind; no one is left out. As everyone is a priest, so everyone is spiritually gifted.

The doctrine of the gifts of the Spirit clarifies a key point. While we are all priests, we do not all have the same priestly ministry. "There are varieties of gifts, but the same Spirit; and there are varieties of services, but the same Lord; and there are varieties of activities, but it is the same God who activates all of them in everyone. To each is given the manifestation of the Spirit for the common good" (1 Cor 12:4-7). There is one universal priesthood, but diverse gifts.

This is the beauty of Christian community! Socially and politically speaking, this is the most radical teaching in Scripture because it says that *no one*—only the Holy Spirit—is authorized to determine who receives which gifts. As we look at Christian movements down through history, we see the amazing way God has raised up the most unlikely of leaders (from a worldly viewpoint). Repeatedly society has expressed the same puzzlement we find in Acts 4:13: "When they saw the boldness of Peter and John and realized that they were uneducated and ordinary men, they were amazed and recognized them as companions of Jesus." This was the only explanation the Jewish leaders could find: These troublemakers had hung out with Jesus.

The Bible is explicit in both testaments that this is precisely God's strategy. As Paul summarized it in 1 Corinthians:

> Consider your own call, brothers and sisters: not many of you were wise by human standards, not many were powerful, not many were of noble birth. But God chose what is foolish in the world to shame the wise; God chose what is weak in the world to shame the strong; God chose what is low and despised in the world, things that are not, to reduce to nothing things that are, so that no one might boast. (1:26-29)

This is true generally, and it is true specifically with the gifts of the Spirit. So in the New Testament we see that God has ordained a whole variety of gifts and ministries. All Christians are gifted, but not all have the same ministry.

How then are we to understand the role of what the church usually calls "ordained ministry"? The key passage is Ephesians 4:11-13. The Lord Jesus ordained a diversity of gifts so that "some would be apostles, some prophets, some evangelists, some pastors and teachers, to equip the saints for the work of ministry, for building up the body of Christ, until all of us come to the unity of the faith and of the knowledge of the Son of God."

The third pillar supporting the biblical doctrine of ministry is the call to be servants of Jesus Christ. In the Old Testament we read of people like "Moses the servant of God" or "David the servant of the Lord." But now, in the New Covenant in Jesus Christ, we are *all* God's servants. We are *all* called to servanthood—to what the New Testament calls *diakonia.*

The call to be servants and ministers of Jesus Christ teaches another key truth. It reveals the *spirit*, the attitude and character, the incarnational manner in which ministry is to be carried out. Jesus' words, "As the Father has sent me, *so* I send you" (John 20:21, italics added), were not meant for the first apostles only. They are the model for all ministry in the name of Jesus Christ.[14]

Here then is our commission to ministry. We are all—each one of us—called as *priests* of God, *gifted* by the Spirit, and sent as *servants* of Jesus Christ.

We may view this comprehensive call of God—the call to specific ministry—as a *fourth circle* within the calls to earth stewardship, to covenant peoplehood, and to the kingdom of God.

The Call to Holiness: Trinitarian Love

We come now to the flaming heart of our concern today, and the heart of the good news: *God's call to holiness.* This is the call to know God in his fullness; to enter into the fellowship of Triune, self-giving love.

This is the call—and the amazing, gracious invitation—to "participate in the divine nature" (2 Pet 1:4 NIV)—to know the Holy Trinity, Father, Son, and Holy Spirit, who allows us to enter into gracious fellowship with him such as otherwise we cannot even imagine. God "has given us . . . his precious and very great promises, so that through them [we] may escape from the corruption that is in the world because of lust, and may become participants of the divine nature" (2 Pet 1:4). Mind-blowing as it sounds, holiness means sharing the very character of God—communion with the Trinity. This is precisely what Jesus prayed for in John 17:

Holy Father, protect them in your name that you have given me, so that they may be one, as we are one. . . . Sanctify them in the truth; your word is truth. As you have sent me into the world, so I have sent them into the world. And for their sakes I sanctify myself, so that they also may be sanctified in truth.

I ask not only on behalf of these, but also on behalf of those who will believe in me through their word, that they may all be one. As you, Father, are in me and I am in you, may they also be in us, so that the world may believe that you have sent me. The glory that you have given me I have given them, so that they may be one, as we are one, I in them and you in me, that they may become completely one, so that the world may know that you have sent me and have loved them even as you have loved me. (John 17:11, 17-23)

Here Jesus beautifully blends the call to holiness, participation in Trinitarian love, and mission in the world. This is what true biblical holiness, understood within the five calls of God, really means! The call to holiness is to be understood within the larger story of the other four calls—because God is one and his plan is one.

A *key reason*, in fact, for the call to holiness is *so that* we can faithfully and graciously fulfill the other four calls. These earlier calls give us a fuller understanding of larger context and the *ethical* and *missional implications* of holiness—what it really can mean to pursue what Wesley called "all inward and outward holiness."

Let us consider, then. What would it mean for us, for the church, empowered by the Spirit and inspired by the example of Jesus and "all the saints," to live out the manifold call of God in postmodern society, and globally?

Holiness and Earth Stewardship

This is most fully understood in the context of the call to holiness. The creation-care mandate is an integral part of the heart call of God. The more we share the character of God, the more we are concerned with God's concerns. So we want to fulfill the call first given to Adam and Eve to tend the garden. We want to preserve, nurture, and protect the physical environment, playing our part in helping it thrive to the glory of God and for his creative, esthetic, and redemptive purposes—as well as for our own survival!

What does earth stewardship lived to the glory of God mean today, in practical terms? It means everything from recycling paper and plastics and caring for church property according to good environmental principles here locally, to supporting efforts to protect endangered species and combat global warming and the disasters it is bringing to the world's poor. Consuming less energy and supporting public policies that help protect God's good earth—this is practical holiness. These are not mere secondary or peripheral ethical concerns, nor are they primarily political issues. They are good old-fashioned holiness issues.

Can we develop Jesus communities that practice creation care? Of course we can! It is simply a matter of the vision and the will. We can show once again in history that we can be God's people in God's land, practicing the principles of Jubilee.

Creation care means, as well, the care of our bodies as part of holy and holistic living—a theme strongly emphasized by John Wesley, E. Stanley Jones, J. C. McPheeters, and Frank Bateman Stanger, among many others. Our bodies were created by God, as were marriage and the family, so these are part of our earth-stewardship mandate.[15]

Holy people are those who feel deeply about all the creatures God has made. We notice a curious thing about the great saints of God, even some who were very otherworldly and saw little value in material things. Many of them saw God manifest in nature and were very sensitive to the well-being or the suffering of all living creatures. Francis of Assisi and John Wesley are, of course, prime examples.

So, holy people tread lightly and joyfully on the earth. Living in reciprocal harmony with God, they seek to live in harmonious reciprocity with God's good land. In our age when we are learning the mysteries of earth and space as never before, we should be even better in our applied holiness in the sphere of earth stewardship than the church has been in the past.

Holiness and Covenant Peoplehood

Here the implications of holiness are quite obvious. We are called to holy, loving, covenant community, and it is the sanctifying Spirit of God who makes this possible.

Covenant peoplehood reminds us that holiness, while personal, is not first of all *individual.* It is primarily *social,* as Wesley insisted. That is, it concerns the character of the Christian community, and of each of our

lives within it. Thus sanctification is not in the first instance the sanctification of the *individual person* but the sanctification of the body of
Christ. As Jesus' physical body on earth was holy, so the body of Christ
on earth is to be holy—loving God with all its heart, mind, soul, and
strength, and loving its earthly neighbors as itself. Holiness therefore
means loving, mutually accountable community, the sanctification of the
body of Christ. This is the key to maintaining our own individual moral
and ethical integrity.[16]

The New Testament says this in many places, but perhaps nowhere
more plainly than in Ephesians 5:18-21: "Be filled with the Spirit,
addressing one another in psalms and hymns and spiritual songs,
singing and making melody to the Lord with all your heart, giving
thanks always and for everything to God the Father in the name of our
Lord Jesus Christ, submitting to one another out of reverence for
Christ" (ESV). Jesus calls us to live in community with God and one
another because God wants to share his very loving, holy, compassion-
ate, merciful, gracious, outreaching self with us—thus to make us like
himself, like Jesus Christ.

Practical holiness as a matter of covenant peoplehood therefore
means attention to the priorities and structures of biblical *koinonia*—
building healthy, holy, and just community. It means affirming the gifts
and fruit of the Spirit; practicing ministry and mission as taught in
Scripture and modeled by Jesus Christ. Thus through the Holy Spirit we
will find ourselves actually fulfilling Jesus' words that his followers would
"also do the works that I do and, in fact, will do greater works than
these, because I am going to the Father" (John 14:12). We will find ourselves fulfilling Jesus' call to serve others, not just ourselves, and we will
see that this is rooted in the very character of God. The more we understand the meaning of the Trinity and Jesus' incarnation, the more we see
that holy love (true Christianity) is all about relinquishing status for the
sake of lifting others.

Christians are to be specialists in building covenant community to the glory of God. In regeneration we receive the very life of God so that we may do this. Building healthy missional community is in fact a major focus of New Testament teaching. Note how much of the New Testament is devoted, *not* to exhortations or strategies for evangelism or mission, but to building community that truly is the body of Christ. Why is this? Because the biblical writers knew that covenant communities that truly incarnate the character of Jesus Christ would in fact do Jesus' work and fulfill God's mission in the world. It is that simple and that profound.

Holiness and the Reign of God

Holiness people are kingdom of God people—if they are biblically grounded. Our kingdom vocation means living for God's larger global and eternal purposes. As the missionary C. T. Studd wrote, "Only one life; 'twill soon be past—only what's done for Christ [and his kingdom] will last." Holiness in a postmodern age means holy, healthy living for the sake of the kingdom of God.

Holiness means living the reality of God's reign *now* in this present age. This was the great new insight that came to E. Stanley Jones in the 1930s. Jones was raised in the holiness tradition; he was a holiness missionary. But after visiting Russia in the heady days of communism's utopian vision, Jones came to realize that he had no adequate theology of the kingdom of God *now*, in *this age*, this present time. He was troubled, and out of that questing came two of Jones' most significant books: *Christ's Alternative to Communism* and *Is the Kingdom of God Realism?* The Christian alternative to communist utopianism, Jones said, is the biblical vision of the kingdom of God. And yes, the kingdom of God is *realism*— the way the world was made to be—not just *idealism* in the sense of some unattainable ideal.[17]

So E. Stanley Jones concluded that the gospel is not only about "the unchanging Christ" but also about "the unshakable kingdom." The gospel concerns a person and a plan—Jesus Christ and his kingdom— and the two must be held together in our theology and in our lived dis- cipleship. This is holiness lived within the sphere, the forward pull, of the kingdom of God. So it must be for us. The work of the sanctifying Spirit is to make us kingdom-of-God people—people who, like Jesus, incarnate the reality and priorities of God's reign in our personal lives, our families, our economics, and our politics.

Holiness and Particular Vocation

The call to holiness is the call to so open ourselves to God's Spirit that his gifts and graces can flow and flourish in our lives. This also is a key part of holiness. Lived holiness is what Hebrews 10:24-25 is talking about: "Let us consider how to provoke one another to love and good deeds, not neglecting to meet together, as is the habit of some, but encouraging one another, and all the more as you see the Day approach- ing." Holiness means life empowered by the Holy Spirit so that what is said of Jesus in John 3:34 becomes true also of his disciples: "The one whom God has sent speaks the words of God, for God gives the Spirit without limit" (NIV).

Holiness means each of us finding our own vocation within, and guided by, the body of Christ. In this way we each make precisely the contribution to God's kingdom purposes that the Spirit intends. Understanding vocation in terms of the larger vision of God's reign, not narrowly in terms of church ministry, is part of the ecclesiological mean- ing of holiness. Our ministry for Jesus Christ is *kingdom* ministry—our whole life and witness in the world—not just *church* ministry.

How do we come to experience this holiness, this deeper life in the Spirit? It comes through receiving the cleansing, empowering presence of the Holy Spirit by faith and obedience. Here pastors, disciplers, and other leaders have a keen responsibility to lead believers into the deeper life in the Spirit.

The Wesleyan emphasis on Christian perfection, or perfecting, holds together two vital emphases at this point. First, the *goal* (the *telos*) of Christian community, and of each of our lives within community, is always to grow up into the fullness of the character of Jesus Christ. This is the central point of Ephesians 4:7-16 and like passages which speak of the church as the body of Christ, animated by and filled with the Spirit.

Second, this walking in the Spirit is to be our *present experience*, not just a future hope. We need to help one another enter into the fullness of the Spirit, to be filled with and walk in the Spirit of Jesus. Generally, as Wesley taught, this deeper dimension of Spirit life comes as a distinct experience subsequent to conversion, though (as Wesley acknowledged) it may be experienced more gradually or less perceptibly—and thus possibly through multiple fresh fillings (or deeper workings) of the Spirit. For most people, it seems, this *process* of growing in the Spirit is enlivened or activated by *crisis* points, more or less perceptible, along the journey.

If our holiness teaching is to be practical and lived, we should not lose this key *crisis and process* link.[18]

As a practical matter of preaching, discipleship, and growth, we need to help believers understand the deeper life of the Spirit that is available to them in Christ. We should give believers opportunities to enter into that deeper life—to confront the dividedness of their own hearts and enter into the fullness, wholeness, and integration *in Christian community* that is our inheritance in Jesus Christ and is a foretaste of that communion we will enjoy in the heavenly kingdom. This was Wesley's concern, and it should be ours.

So this is the call to holiness in relation to the other calls discussed earlier. I emphasize again: It is the Spirit's infilling that supplies the *power*, the *energy*, the effective movemental *impulse* that enables the church and each of us as Jesus' disciples to fulfill the *other* calls God extends to us.

We may view this fifth call of God—the call to holiness—as the *central circle* among all God's calls. This is the heart of our vocation, for it is the call to the heart of God. It is the call to love the Lord our God with all our heart, strength, soul, and mind, and thus to love our neighbors as ourselves. It is the central, the capacitating, the essential equipping call—the call that enables us to live out our gifts and callings; to see and serve God's liberating reign; to be God's covenant people; to care for the good earth. Thus responding willingly to all God's calls, the church and each of us personally glorifies God and serves the world through the gifts Christ bestows (cf. Rom 12; 1 Pet 4:10-11).

This vision is dynamic, not static! It is going somewhere—to the fulfillment of God's mission and the coming of God's reign in all its fullness. It is active and dynamic, for the Spirit draws us forward in mission in the spirit and character of Jesus.

Postmodern Holiness?

How then does the biblical conception of holiness respond to the challenges of postmodernity? First, *holiness is holistic*. It meets the human need for a way of life that reaches all dimensions of our existence. Even though postmodernity is famously hostile to holism and metanarratives, yet people sense the need for an existence that at some deep level is whole.

Second, *holiness is particular*. It recognizes the uniqueness of each person created in God's image; that the Holy Spirit works uniquely in each individual, cleansing, empowering, and granting gifts that particularly fit each person's needs, capacities, and cultural context.

Third, *holiness is narrative*. It is not first of all an abstract idea, philosophy, or theology. It is a story about what God has done for us and how our own stories find meaning but also self-transcendence within the story and personal reality of the Triune God who sent Jesus Christ into the world in the power of the Holy Spirit.

Finally, *holiness is life*. It is experience. It is not first of all a doctrine but first of all a love relationship with God in Jesus Christ and the Spirit. Thus holiness is community—*koinonia* with God and with one another in a new kind of fellowship, the church, which simultaneously lives in two worlds—the one we now see visibly around us, and the one which is to come and which in fact is constantly, invisibly, penetratingly around us right now. Holiness is *undividedness*—the life in which, lost in God, we find ourselves. And thus finding God's love in us, we reach out and find others.[19]

Conclusion

On a warm autumn afternoon, my wife, Jan, called me outside to see something strange. The sun was shining; golden leaves were falling from the hickory trees. I went out and looked, but all I saw was scattered leaves drifting down.

"I see only some leaves falling," I said, "obeying the law of gravity."

"Look higher!" she said. "Way up in the sky."

I looked higher—and saw a phenomenon I had never witnessed before. Thousands of leaves high above our tree, fluttering and floating and drifting away in all directions. Heading up and outward, not down to earth.

"What happened?" I asked.

She said that just minutes earlier a gust of wind had swept up through the tree, driving a cloud of leaves high in the sky where they floated and scattered, not returning to earth. The leaves had conquered the law of gravity by a superior force—a breath of wind that lifted the leaves from the branches and scattered them far and wide.

Aha, I thought. *Now I get it. This is a lesson for the church! How can the church overcome its deadening gravity—the weight of sin, self-centeredness, bureaucracy and institutionalism, rigid and obsolete structures?* There is a way—*the breath of the Spirit of God.* "The wind blows where it chooses, and you hear the sound of it, but you do not know where it comes from or where it goes. So it is with everyone who is born of the Spirit" (John 3:8).

Brothers and sisters, let us look higher!

The five calls of God may seem like demands, but they are really the breath of the Spirit. They not only drive us; they lift us, call us higher, call us to such faithfulness, ministry, love, and joy as has hardly entered our minds and imaginations.

But we have to be open to the Spirit. We have to place ourselves in God's currents. Like those autumn leaves, the church can soar and scatter its witness to the world, in the name of Jesus and the power of the Spirit.

The five calls of God are the compound call of the Spirit. *By the Spirit of the living God,* Jesus-people today can:

- Be filled with all the fullness of God in Christ, living holy, devout, pure, healing lives, being Jesus' counterculture and contrast society in witness to the world
- Exercise a beautiful array of ministries and callings, according to the diversity of the gifts of the Spirit
- Be God's kingdom people in the world, living in full allegiance to Jesus and his reign—Spirit-endowed coworkers for the kingdom of God
- Live as a faithful covenant people, building accountable community, growing up into Jesus Christ, embodying the spirit of God's law in holy love
- Care for the garden, this good earth, God's gift in trust to us, working in faith, hope, and confidence for the healing of all creation, being the leading edge among the nations for the care and feeding and eventual reconciliation of all things—things visible and invisible; things in heaven and on earth (e.g., Eph 1:10, 22; 3:9; Col 1:16-20; Heb 1:2-3)

This is what holiness—life in the Spirit in response to the fivefold call of God—means in a postmodern world and within earth's diverse cultures. We must be a holy people. For God says, it is "not by might, nor by power, but by my Spirit" (Zech 4:6 ESV) that he fulfills his designs.

In faithful response to the fivefold call of God we learn more fully what the words mean: "They who wait for the LORD shall renew their strength; / they shall mount up with wings like eagles; / they shall run and not be weary; / they shall walk and not faint" (Isa 40:31 ESV).

CHAPTER FIVE

THE PRIESTHOOD OF ALL BELIEVERS IN THE POSTMODERN CONGREGATION

Robert G. Tuttle Jr.

A part from *sola fide* and *sola scriptura*, the priesthood of all believers is the signal doctrine of the Protestant Reformation. Previously, ordained priests alone had increasingly done the work of the parish. They interpreted Scripture, heard confession, assigned penances, pronounced absolution, and managed the general affairs of the church. Unfortunately, many seminaries (although few would admit it) instruct their students as to the history of this important doctrine without teaching them this indispensable lesson: they cannot do ministry alone. This is one of the primary reasons why, today, it is not uncommon for pastors to burn out during their first two to five years of ministry. The Bible clearly teaches that every person, every part of the body of Christ, has a sphere of influence; every Christian has a role in the ministry of the church. In fact, ministry has two dominant themes—call and community. Look for these to set the tone as we turn first to history and theology, then to two important biblical texts.

History and Theology

The Early Church

The early church was obviously a lay movement. As important as I believe ordination to be, I (and others) have always been a bit hard put to make the case for ordination from the Bible alone, especially the New Testament. In fact, passages like Revelation 1:6; 5:10; and 20:6 seem to suggest a broader understanding of priesthood.[1]

Since Pentecost the church has struggled with the roles of its leadership and membership. The problem seems to be a lack of understanding and balance. In *The Call*, Os Guinness writes about a "Catholic Distortion" and a "Protestant Distortion." The Catholic distortion tends to elevate the spiritual at the expense of the secular so that ministry is only for the ordained: *ministry* is just another word for "ordination." The Protestant counterpart elevates the secular at the expense of the spiritual so that everything is secular: *ordination* is just another word for "work." Edward Schillebeeckx suggests that balance between an "ontological sacerdotalist" view of ministry on the one hand and a purely "functionalist" view on the other, can only be achieved by a theological view of the church's ministry as a charismatic office that functions within the community, in service to the community, and confirmed by the community (both men and women).[2] History teaches the need for balance so that priesthood is a holy calling for all of the church's several ministries to be shared by clergy and laity alike. The earliest lessons come from the earliest church.

Although a few (such as the seven in Acts 6:1-7) were *appointed* by the apostles with the laying on of hands, the ministry of the early church was done by ordinary Christians. Admittedly, Paul and Barnabas were *commissioned* with prayer, fasting, and the laying on of hands (Acts 13:3), but all Christians born of the Spirit were supposedly gifted for ministry within their own spheres of influence. If Christianity were to affect the world, men and women would have to walk the roads, board the ships, face the mobs, endure the prisons, and pray for the good of the cause.

It is significant that the call to ministry has always been inclusive. From the beginning women and men needed to be faithful within their various spheres of influence. Again, community has always been important. We have never been able to do it alone. Several years ago I read Richard Leakey's *People of the Lake.*[3] Although anthropological theory has advanced much since Leakey wrote this in 1978, his observations still pack a powerful truth. Leakey's theory is that between 1.2 and 1.5 million years ago, four strains of humankind were evolving simultaneously. It was thought that the strain that evolved into modern humankind was a macho strain—the ones that ran around smiting themselves upon the chest—the survival of the fittest. The discovery was that those strains were the first to become extinct. The reason? They were loners and they got picked off. The only strain that survived to evolve into modern humankind was *Homo sapiens*. The reason? *Homo sapiens* was the only strain that dared to become community—they watched each other's backs. Margaret Mead insists that civilization was in place at least from the date of the earliest discovered human fossil with a healed broken femur. The only way to survive a broken femur is for someone else to feed you.

Perhaps the greatest precedent established by the first few generations of the church is that *ministry was an inclusive community affair*— no one could do it alone. Community was only part of the equation, however. Even more important is that they not only relied on each other, *they relied upon God*. The history of the Israelites teaches us this lesson time and again. Although the Israelites understood community, they always floundered when they relied on anyone or anything other than the I AM God.

For the first 150 years of the Christian movement, every Christian was a priest. Then, for the next 150 years, most lay Christians continued to take the Great Commandment and the Great Commission as a personal mandate to Christian ministry. The great Ambrose of Milan (339–397) was an unbaptized layperson until *after* he was elected—*by the laity*—Bishop of Milan.

When not being sacrificed on the "altars of amusement," early Christians were busy spreading and doing the work of the gospel. Since most believed that the return of Christ was imminent, the time was short. They had no time to waste. The darkness of the hour served only to increase the urgency of their appeal. Whether in home or marketplace, men, women, even children were busy chattering and then living the gospel. What could possibly exact such risk?

"Praise, glory, and honor" were important words in the Epistles of Peter. Find them here nestled in a text that offers hope in the midst of the din:

> Praise be to the God and Father of our Lord Jesus Christ! In his great mercy he has given us new birth into a living hope through the resurrection of Jesus Christ from the dead, and into an inheritance that can never perish, spoil or fade—kept in heaven for you, who through faith are shielded by God's power *until the coming of the salvation that is ready to be revealed in the last time.* In this you greatly rejoice, though now *for a little while you may have had to suffer grief in all kinds of trials.* These have come so that your faith—of greater worth than gold, which perishes even though refined by fire—may be proved genuine and may result in praise, glory and honor *when Jesus Christ is revealed.* (1 Pet 1:3-7 NIV; emphasis added)

Common, ordinary folks were encouraged by such words. They had been transformed into the kind of people who took them seriously—dead seriously. As they moved about town and country, every encounter seemed an opportunity to speak and demonstrate the words of a living hope. This was not mindless frenzy. It was low-key, but intentional. It was unscripted, but anticipated. It was winsome, but intelligent. It was the result of prayer. It was the work of the Spirit. It was ministry at its best.

In his *City of God*, Augustine wrote, "Ordination does not make a priest, but a servant of a priest . . . a servant and an officer of the common priesthood." [4] Whenever ordained clergy sought to horde or control the gifts intended for the ministry the church, the church was never what God intended it to be. This came to a head during the Protestant Reformation.

The Reformation

During the Reformation Martin Luther wrote regarding the true priestly office. One can find quotations relevant to this in every volume of his *Works*. Let me give you a few examples:

> Faith must do everything. It alone is the true priestly office and permits no one else to take its place. Therefore all Christians are priests; the men, priests, the women, priestesses, be they young or old, masters or servants, mistresses or maids, learned or unlearned. Here there is no difference, unless faith be unequal. [5]

> Let every one, therefore, who knows himself to be a Christian be assured of this, and apply it to himself—that we are all priests, and there is no difference between us; that is to say, we have the same power in respect to the Word and sacraments. However, no one may make use of this power except by *the consent of the community or by the call of a superior.* [6]

Lest one think that Luther did not appreciate ordination, however, read on:

> For what is the common property of all, no individual may arrogate to himself, unless he be called. And therefore this sacrament of ordination, if it have any meaning at all, is nothing else than a certain rite whereby one is called to the ministry of the Church. [7]

The point is that, for Luther, God's call was upon both clergy and lay as confirmed by the community to do the ministry of the church. Luther was opposed to those "Roman" sacraments (beyond Baptism and the Eucharist) that were intended only for the few. For example, regarding ordination as sacrament he wrote:

Of this sacrament the church of Christ knows nothing, it is an invention of the church of the pope. Not only is there nowhere any promise of grace attached to it, but there is not a single word said about it in the whole New Testament. Now it is ridiculous to put forth as a sacrament of God something that cannot be proved to have been instituted by God. I do not hold that this rite, which has been observed for so many centuries, should be condemned; but in sacred things I am opposed to the invention of human fictions.[8]

In summary, God calls every Christian to the priesthood and God calls every community of faith to confirm that calling in its several parts.

The Movement Called Methodist

John Wesley, as much as anyone, had an appreciation for lay ministry. The early leaders within the connection of Methodists (apart from the Wesleys and George Whitefield) were laymen (and soon afterward, lay-women). The converts to the preaching of Whitefield and the Wesleys were many. The problem was that when they moved on to preach elsewhere, the people fell away so that, upon return, they were forced to start again, but with less success than before since the second impression was never as strong as the first. Wesley devised a remedy. He would leave a layperson in charge (since no clergy would assist at all). For example, Thomas Maxfield was given responsibility for the society in London and was instructed to confirm the newly converted by reading, by praying, or by exhortation. Wesley then watched his lay exhorters turn into lay preachers. Maxfield's biographer writes: "Being fervent in spirit, and mighty in the Scriptures, he greatly profited the people. They crowded to hear him; and, by the increase of their number, as well as by their earnest and deep attention, they insensibly led him to go farther than he had first designed. He began to *preach*."[9]

Upon his return to London, Wesley was at first distressed, thinking that Mr. Maxfield had overstepped his bounds. An interesting exchange ensued with his mother, Susanna, who was then living in a house next to the Foundry. Wesley stated rather curtly, "Thomas Maxfield has turned preacher, I find." His mother, looking at him seriously, replied: "John, you know what my sentiments have been; you cannot suspect me of favoring readily anything of this kind; but take care what you do with respect to that young man, for he is as surely *called of God* to preach as you are. Examine what have been the fruits of his preaching and hear him also yourself."[10]

It is interesting that ten years into the revival Wesley would no longer preach in the open air unless a society was already in place to minister to the awakened. Wesley typically walked the streets of a small English town singing hymns with an entourage of 20 to 30 people, letting a crowd draw. They would march to the town center; Wesley would usually climb the steps to the market cross and preach a fifteen-minute sermon on death or hell. This was pre-evangelism. The invitation was not to accept Christ but to fear God and flee the wrath to come. The entourage would then circulate among those responding to that invitation, signing them up on the spot for a class meeting that afternoon. Seventy percent of those won to Jesus in the eighteenth-century Evangelical Revival were won to Jesus Christ one-on-one in lay-led class meetings.

One can quickly see that common to both the Continental and English Reformations were the importance of call and the confirmation of the community. Just as ministers developed out of a grassroots laity, it appears abundantly clear that we need to be aware of those being called out of the rank and file. We can exhort and affirm those gifts around us so that the whole body, the church, might be duly strengthened.

This is not to disparage ordination in the least. Rather, it is important to realize that ministry is the responsibility of every Christian. Nowhere is that better demonstrated than in the Bible.

Two Biblical Texts

Ephesians 4

Ephesians 4 speaks of Christ making the gifts of the Spirit available to all. Although there are many texts that are relevant (such as the

"Farewell Discourse" in John 13:31–16:33, where Jesus bequeaths the same Spirit at work in him over the past three years to his disciples), Ephesians 4 is important in that it reminds us that the gifts of the Spirit are "to prepare God's people for works of service, so that the body of Christ may be built up until we all reach unity in the faith and in the knowledge of the Son of God and become mature, attaining to the whole measure of the fullness of Christ" (vv. 12-13 NIV).

There is no general outpouring of the Holy Spirit under the old covenant. The Spirit cannot reign where sin still reigns. In the Old Testament God anoints specific persons for specific tasks. By virtue of what God has done in Jesus, however, the gifts are now available to the church and all of its parts. The Spirit gives these (and other) gifts to the church: apostles, prophets, evangelists, pastors, and teachers. These gifts equip God's people to do the work and build up the church—the body of Christ—in love.

1 Corinthians 12

This text makes similar points but speaks more to the diversity of gifts equipping the parts of the body, especially those that seem to be weaker. I frequently tell local churches that no one pastor can be most effective to more that 10 percent of the people. If one pastor is the only one doing ministry in the church then 90 percent of the needs are not being met. So how do we meet all of the needs? Everyone gets in on the fun. Lay people do not pay pastors to receive their birthrights—their spheres of influence.

> Now the body is not made up of one part but of many. If the foot should say, "Because I am not a hand, I do not belong to the body," it would not for that reason cease to be part of the body. . . . The eye cannot say to the hand, "I don't need you!" And the head cannot say to the feet, "I don't need you!" On the contrary, those parts of the body that seem to be weaker are *indispensable*. (1 Cor 12:14-15, 21-22 NIV, emphasis added)

On the practical side, let me make just a few points in light of the churches we serve. First, I cannot tell you how much mischief enters the fray when pastors have a need to be in control and consequently get overworked to the point of burnout. In a series of lectures entitled "Fired Up or Burned Out?" I speak about people supporting what they help create. Too many pastors seek to train their lay people only to support their own programs rather than equipping, enabling, and discipling for the vision of the whole.

I am weary of pastors going into churches with the answers before they understand the questions. I have a student who has been coordinating lay ministry for years and insists that building ministry teams empowers shared leadership so that lay and clergy are together making leadership decisions in a way that is deeper than simply reaching a consensus.

All of the gifts of the Spirit are intended for the church, not for any one individual. The gifts are to enable the various body parts to minister effectively in their own spheres of influence. Since our spheres are different, our gifts are different. I do not covet your gifts. You do not covet mine. And we both refuse to go poaching.

Second, it occurs to me that, in order for the appointive system to work in my own denomination (where pastors change more or less frequently), the church must have a strong lay base to sustain the vision and energy from one year to the next. That was the genius of the circuit rider system in early Methodism. Until the circuit rider was "located" or appointed to one location the work of the church was sustained by the laity. Classes were lay led. Sermons were lay preached. The church's ministry, whether feeding, clothing, or visiting, was lay initiated.[11]

Finally, let me say a brief word about barriers to lay ministry. One, *we lack motivation*. We simply do not understand what is at stake. God is sending us to "open their eyes and turn them from darkness to light, and from the power of Satan to God, so that they may receive forgiveness of sins and a place among those who are sanctified by faith in [Jesus]" (Acts 26:17-18 NIV). Two, *we fear rejection*. We do not realize that it takes many different witnesses before any real encounter with God takes place and that inherent to ministry is far more rejection than affirmation—the nos, however, are just as important as the yesses. Get over it! Do not take it personally! Three, *we assume inadequacy*. We do not realize that our greatest strengths are anointed weaknesses. Our weaknesses, perhaps more than our strengths, establish our greatest spheres of influence. Some ordained types do ministry "too well" to be effective in some lay spheres.

Conclusion

Sue Mallory in her book *The Equipping Church* writes of equipping principles not as add-on programs but as core values that remind us of God's call upon all of our lives.[12] Furthermore, we must always remember that God will not call us without also equipping us. I have always been fascinated by the exchange between Jesus and Peter in Matthew 16:

> I tell you that you are Peter, and on this rock I will build *my* church, and the gates of Hades will not overcome it. I will give *you* the keys of the kingdom of heaven; whatever *you* bind on earth will be bound in heaven, and whatever *you* loose on earth will be loosed in heaven. (vv. 18-19 NIV, emphasis added)

One problem with the church is that we think the church is *our* responsibility and the *kingdom* is God's responsibility. This text states the exact opposite. When Jesus refers to "you," he is using the plural form, "you all," to refer to the disciples as a whole and, by extension, the church. The church belongs to God while *we*, the church, have the keys to the kingdom. The church is not like the body of Christ, the church *is* the body of Christ (1 Cor 12:12). No metaphor is intended. God could obviously do it without us, but has chosen not to. If ministry is going to take place in this age, ministry is going to take place through folks like us or not at all. Either we fully understand the priesthood of *all* believers or God will simply return in all God's glory and claim God's own out of the rubble.

Living with the Tension: Holiness versus Grace in Postmodern Ministry

Charles E. Gutenson

The terms *grace* and *holiness* each have a rather narrow range of uses within Scripture and within the broader Christian tradition. For example, within the Methodist tradition, we may have heard the term *grace* used in such phrases as "the means of grace," often deployed to reference the sacraments. I suspect many of us have heard grace defined as "unmerited favor"; so that to say "God is gracious" is, in essence, to say that God loves and blesses without regard to our deserving it. The term *holiness* often refers to an external quality of a thing whereby it is designated and set apart for God's purposes. This sense of holiness is often characterized as "ceremonial holiness." On the other hand, holiness is sometimes used to reference an inner quality relating to the moral and ethical goodness of a thing. This latter sense finds its highest expression in God's own nature, overtly expressed when Scripture asserts that God is holy.

Given my particular interests here, let me immediately set aside the notion of ceremonial holiness so that I can focus instead on holiness as moral and ethical goodness. This is because, first, it has been widely argued that, over time, the idea of ceremonial holiness has been lost in favor of the more typical sense of moral and ethical goodness. Second, Wesleyans concerned with the doctrine of sanctification or holiness are naturally drawn to that sense of holiness relating explicitly to our living the life that pleases God. Similarly, with regard to the concept of grace, while I shall offer some attention to both the concepts of grace as used in the phrase "the means of grace" and in the sense of "unmerited favor," my focus will lie elsewhere. I plan to focus more on the notion of grace as empowerment to live the life that pleases God.

These statements already point to the thesis for which I will be arguing in this essay. I want to demonstrate that God gives grace for the express purpose of empowering the life that pleases God. This is a life in which the new has come and the old has passed away, a life characterized by holiness. For this reason, grace must not be deployed as a term suggesting our getting off the hook, but rather as a reference to power for transformation. When seen this way, grace can never be a lowest common denominator quite simply because it expects too much. Get off the hook, we do, but only because, in a very real sense, the old "on the hook" person is no longer who we are. Consequently, empowering grace and holiness can never truly stand in tension, since the former is related to the latter as cause and effect. In other words, as we receive grace from God we are empowered to be able to live as God intends. In defending my thesis, I will examine each of these major concepts, grace and holiness, as well as their interaction with each other.

Grace

It is fair and accurate to claim that we, as humans, would be in sorry shape if grace were not bestowed on us by God without regard to merit.

If we had to somehow *earn* grace before it was given to us by God, it is difficult to see how we could ever be the recipients of God's grace. Hence, there must be an aspect of grace that can be characterized as unmerited favor. Nevertheless, at some point we have to move beyond thinking of the free nature of grace and ask ourselves: *What end does God have in mind when he bestows grace on us? Does God intend it merely as an expression of God's forgiveness of our sinful behavior? Is it intended primarily to be a gift which sets us in right relationship without any attendant expectations? Or, is there a deeper purpose?* Of course, I have already provided the answer: God grants us grace to empower us to live the life that pleases God.

John Wesley's thought, especially his articulation of the concept of grace within his order of salvation, is helpful here. Wesley spoke of five different kinds of grace that God makes available to humans (actually, I prefer to think of them as five different *functions* of divine grace rather than thinking of them as actually different *kinds* of grace). These are prevenient grace, convicting grace, justifying grace, sanctifying grace, and glorifying grace. Each one of these takes up an explicit place in Wesley's order of salvation. Let us consider each and see how they demonstrate that grace, first and foremost, ought to be understood as empowerment for initiation into and participation in the life of God.

In an interesting claim regarding his debate with the Calvinists, Wesley once noted that he came within a "hairsbreadth" of Calvinism. Specifically, he agreed with the Calvinists that natural humanity could only sin and that all good works were attributable to God. It would seem, at first glance, that Wesley would have to take the next step and affirm with the Calvinists a doctrine of theological determinism; yet, there was that "hairsbreadth," which prevented him from doing so and that "hairsbreadth" turned out to be the concept of prevenient grace. Rather than placing free will in the created order (humans are inherently free by virtue of their being created as such), Wesley argued that human freedom had to be placed within the salvific order. In other words, after the fall, humans have free will only as a consequence of God's saving acts. Wesley believed that every individual ever born was already the recipient of irresistible, prevenient grace that served to counter some of the effects of original sin and that restored human faculties to the point that humans were enabled to respond freely to God's offer of salvation. The key point is the purpose for which prevenient grace is given, its teleological nature. Prevenient grace is not given to humans *merely in order that they might exercise their wills freely,* but rather *so that they might be freed from their bondage to sin* and, thus, that they might be empowered to respond to God's further offers of grace. Prevenient grace is bestowed on all humanity, but it is given for the express purpose of making possible the return to right relationship with God and within the human family.

The Christian doctrine of original sin, however it is taken, intends to communicate the fact that humanity as it is does not correspond to the divine intention for humanity. To say that humans are sinful or fallen is to affirm this and to point out that humans stand in need of transformation. Of course, if, as we Wesleyans believe, humans are free, then before one can actually *be* transformed, one must *see the need for* transformation. Wesley called *convicting* or *convincing grace* that function of grace that serves to bring to conscious awareness the disparity between the actual human condition and that intended by God. Properly understood, sin is a profoundly relational concept, for it is precisely the relationship between humans and God as well as among humans that is ruptured because of human sin. Consequently, the condition that expresses this disparity between humans as they are and humans as God intended can best be characterized as one of estrangement or alienation. That is, human persons stand estranged or alienated from God and from each other. Convicting grace functions to help us see our sinfulness and the alienation that is its inevitable consequence. Whereas prevenient grace restored a measure of human freedom, convicting grace empowers us as to the wise use of that freedom. In both cases, the empowering nature of God's grace is evident.

Since God intends to transform persons and to restore them to right relationship with himself and with each other, the divine intention could never be satisfied merely through convicting grace. While awareness of the need for transformation precedes the transformative acts themselves, actual transformation must occur if human restoration is to occur. Wesley called that function of grace that begins the process of transformation *justifying grace*. Historically, to set one on the path of participation in the life of God has been characterized by confession of and repentance for one's sins and by the consequent forgiveness of those sins by God, resulting in restoration of broken relationship with God. Now, we must be clear at this point. Justifying grace is not an end in itself, but rather points beyond itself to the *telos* or end that God has in mind for us: conformity to the image of Christ. In a sense, justifying grace and the accompanying conversion comprise merely the beginning of one's journey in the participation in the life of God. Of course, it builds on the functions of grace that preceded, prevenient grace and convicting grace, but it marks a significant point in the transformation process. Just as prevenient grace overcame the worst effects of the fall, thereby enabling human response to God's call, justifying grace changes the person's whole orientation from one closed to God to one open and responsive to further bestowals of grace by God. Justifying grace, as transformation, empowers initial reconciliation and movement into the life that pleases God.

As with empowerment for the change of direction that comes with justifying grace, so we cannot continue our growth as Christians apart from God's grace. Wesley used the term *sanctifying grace* to capture that function of grace whereby we are empowered for the ongoing growth toward God's ultimate goal of conformity to the image of Christ. While justifying grace marks a decisive point in our turn toward God, sanctifying grace engages, guides, and directs us throughout eternity, as we begin a participation in the life of God that never ends. Interestingly, many early church fathers described this process using terms such as *apotheosis* and *deification* whereby they intended to claim that it was the destiny of saved humanity to become as much like God as possible for humans. For this to have concrete meaning, we have to move beyond merely repeating the phrase "be conformed to the image of Christ," and at some point inquire what such a life would look like. When we discuss *holiness*, below, we shall have more to say about this; for now, though, we merely note the extent to which grace needs to be understood as empowerment. Here, it is empowerment to live in—as Wesley called it, "Christian perfection." How else could one conceive this except as empowerment to be holy?

Given what I have said thus far, I can be quite brief with regard to *glorifying grace*, for it is, to use Paul's words, that function of grace that allows "this mortal body [to] put on immortality" (1 Cor 15:53 ESV). It references that final act whereby God transforms us from merely human, corruptible creatures to the incorruptible creatures that will live with him throughout eternity. In a sense, then, glorifying grace can be seen as empowerment to live forever in the divine presence.

We can see, then, that each of these functions of divine grace is intended to bring about some state of affairs or to accomplish certain ends. As might be expected, each type of grace realizes empowerment in somewhat different ways. Prevenient grace involves God's deploying his power to overcome the damage done to human volitional faculties pursuant to the fall. Convicting grace challenges our way of viewing the world and empowers us to see the world in a whole new way. Justifying grace empowers us for initiation into participation in the life of God so that a whole new relationship with God, mediated through the Holy Spirit, follows. Sanctifying grace empowers the ongoing growth in our participation in the divine life. And glorifying grace involves empowering us to live in God's actual presence. In some cases, the term *empowerment* takes on more the character of the presentation of a possibility for human response, and in others, more the character of an actual application of God's transforming power. In each case, though, Wesley's categories of grace ought to be understood as God's active presence in our lives leading us ever deeper into the divine life and bringing us ever closer to living out the life that pleases God. In short, grace ought first and foremost to be understood as empowerment for the sake of living lives that are characterized as "holy." What, then, does it mean to "be holy"?

Holiness

"I, the Lord your God, am holy." We need not look very hard to find this affirmation within the biblical texts, and it seems straightforward enough from the frequency and nature of the occurrences that *holy* is not merely one of many interchangeable descriptors that one might apply to God, but is rather an expression of the very nature of God. Further, while the term is also used in reference to things other than God, it seems clear that holiness is intimately connected to God's nature so that anything else that might be considered holy is regarded as holy only in relation to God.

In Leviticus 19:2, God tells Moses to say to the people, "You shall be holy, for I the LORD your God am holy." Here, the affirmation that God is holy is coupled very closely with certain expectations that God has for his hearers. Specifically, God does not merely affirm his own holiness but also states explicitly his intention that humans be imitators of God precisely with regard to God's holiness. This makes all the more pressing our interest in determining what it means to be holy, and the subsequent content of Leviticus 19 begins to flesh out what God means by his command that we be holy. Importantly, the characteristics of holiness laid out here can be summarized by what Jesus called the two great commandments: love the Lord your God with all your heart, mind, soul, and strength; and love your neighbor as yourself. Consider just a few examples from Leviticus 19:

- Honor your parents. (v. 3)
- Keep the Lord's sabbath. (v. 3)

- Do not worship anything other than the Lord your God.
- During harvest time, for grain or grapes, leave some for the poor and sojourner. (vv. 9-10)
- Treat others with integrity (no lying, cheating, stealing).
- Welcome the strangers in your land. (vv. 33-34)
- Make fair and impartial judgments. (vv. 15-16)
- Do not take advantage of another, even if you can.
- Love your neighbor as yourself.
- Remember to give to God the appropriate praise and sacrifice.

Interestingly, between sets of commands, the statement appears, "I am the LORD your God," as if to remind the reader at every turn that the commands themselves are rooted in the very nature of the God who is characterized first and foremost in this passage as the Holy One. To live the life that pleases God, that is to be holy, is to live out these commands and others like them.

If we move forward to the New Testament, at the end of the first section of the Sermon on the Mount, we find Jesus issuing the following injunction to his hearers: "You, therefore, must be perfect, as your heavenly Father is perfect" (Matt 5:48 RSV). Once again, we see the divine call to human life to be imitators of God—that is, what God intends humans to be is rooted in his own nature. The term Jesus used here is a form of the Greek word *telos*, which carries ideas such as "end" or "purpose" or "completion," and as noted in the RSV and other translations, the idea of "perfection." Wesley, when speaking of the doctrine of holiness could use such phrases as "entire sanctification" (and, of course, the underlying sense of "sanctification" is a state of holiness) and "Christian perfection." Consequently, while the underlying Greek word for "perfection" is not the Greek term usually translated "holy" or "holiness," it seems clear that the surrounding context in Matthew 5 carries with it the sense of moral or ethical purity that is rooted in the divine nature. It does not seem much of a stretch, then, to argue that Jesus' call in the Sermon on the Mount is a New Testament form of Yahweh's Old Testament call for humans to be holy.

It is important to note that, if we examine the entirety of Matthew 5, we will find that the call to be perfect can be reduced to the two great commandments just as we saw in Leviticus 19. In short, the life that pleases God and that lives out faithfully the holiness to which we are called is a life that orients itself properly to our Creator (i.e., we love God with all our heart, mind, soul, and strength) and, likewise, orients itself properly to the other. In other words, we are to love our neighbors as ourselves. However, it is particularly noteworthy that in the immediate context of Matthew 5:43-48 we find that the divine perfection is directly connected with loving and blessing others *without regard to merit*. In fact, this "loving without regard to merit" is to go as far as loving our enemies and praying for our persecutors. The extent to which this is rooted in the imitation of God is obvious once we begin to think it through: while we were yet hostile to God, God sent his son; while the soldiers persecuted Jesus on the cross, he prayed for their forgiveness; and the very act of incarnation itself is an act whereby the Son reaches out beyond the divine life to offer himself to and for his human creatures. If we are on the right path here, then to be holy, to live the life that pleases God, is to orient ourselves beyond ourselves in order to love God and our fellows with utter abandon.

We can take one further step. If we were to push the question of what it means to be an imitator of God to its limits, I believe that we would ultimately find the proper resting place for understanding the imitation of God is the doctrine of the Trinity. The Trinitarian doctrine intends to affirm that, at the bedrock of reality, there exist three persons in relationships of perfectly self-giving love. The early fathers thought this so profound that they described it by saying that the Father gives himself, wholly and without reservation, to the Son and the Spirit; the Son gives himself, wholly and without reservation to the Father and the Spirit; and the Spirit gives himself, wholly and without reservation, to the Father and the Son. This describes a depth of interrelationality that extends well beyond the limits of how we normally think, but not, I believe, beyond the limits of the divine intent for us. In fact, many argue, and I think them correct, that when Scripture affirms that we are created in God's image, it is most preeminently affirming our being created as relational beings. What all of this leads us to, in the end, is a recognition that holiness is first and foremost a relational notion so that to be holy, to live out the divine intent for human life together, is to stand in right relation to God and to our fellows. That right relationship toward God is one of love and adoration; that right relationship toward each other is the self-giving love that constitutes an imitation of the inner life of the Triune God.

This brings us back to our original thesis, that grace, properly understood, is empowerment to live the life that pleases God, i.e., to be holy. We have examined Wesley's way of characterizing grace to better understand what it means to speak of grace as an empowering reality. We then turned our attention to the term *holiness* in effort to grasp the end goal of empowering grace, that is, to understand the characteristics of a life of holiness. At this point, we could reframe our thesis: Grace, properly understood, is empowerment to live out the life that pleases God, a life characterized by love of God and love of fellow humans with a self-giving love that gives freely to others without regard to merit.

When so understood, there can be no tension between grace and holiness. Similarly, when matters are taken this way, holiness can never be reduced to a list of simple do's and don'ts, for the call to the level of relationship we have discovered implied by the call to holiness is far too complicated and context-dependent for that. May we be the happy recipients of such grace and may it empower us to live according to the divine intent.

Relating Grace and Holiness: Tensions?

Before we draw our reflections to a conclusion, one further point requires our attention. Although I have argued that there can be no tension between grace and holiness properly understood, we frequently hear reference to such a tension, and hence we must consider what gives rise to this common sentiment.

First, it is worth noting that the tensions we often see in relating grace and holiness seem to arise in particular when we think of grace and holiness within the context of shared human life—that is, within the context of our interactions with each other. Does not being gracious imply being nonjudgmental and accepting of each other? On the other hand, does not our rightful expectation of holiness being manifested in each other's lives imply that we need to make judgments and demand accountability? When we begin to think of matters in this way, an apparent tension between grace and holiness becomes evident, one pole seemingly tending toward unquestioning acceptance and the other toward conditioning acceptance too harshly. If I am correct in my argument that there is no tension between grace and holiness, then how do we explain this?

Of course, I have only argued that there is no tension between grace and holiness *when they both are properly understood*. When either grace or holiness is not properly understood, tensions are almost sure to rise. I wonder if the error that most commonly leads to misconceptions concerning grace and holiness is not primarily a failure to grasp adequately the close interrelationship between the two such that the former, grace, has the latter, holiness, as its purpose and goal. Recall that we have argued that grace is empowerment to *be* holy. However, whenever grace is separated from its purpose of empowerment, it can too easily tend toward a facile acceptance. Grace, as we have argued, is not mere acceptance without regard to merit, but rather acceptance without regard to merit *for the purpose of transformation*. Additionally, when we think of grace as separated from holiness as its goal, any sense of accountability to actually *become* holy is easily lost. On the other hand, when holiness is seen as the goal of grace, our extension of grace to others will be driven by our longing to see the other live the life that pleases God, and this will carry with it space for the appropriate accountability structures. When either of these aspects of grace is lost, it can appear that grace indulges, if not actually affirms, our failure to be holy.

Similar problems can arise in our understanding from the side of holiness. When holiness is separated from its relationality expressed in love of God and neighbor, it easily becomes an abstract affirmation of certain rules rooted, at best, in some arbitrary conception of divine command theory. This leads to a "rules based" understanding of holiness that is severed from its proper justification and that too easily ignores contextual complexities. We are told that we are to do X or not to do Y, but we do not really understand why. Hence, we condemn those who do not do X or do Y, but we cannot give any basis other than "God said so." Holiness as the life lived in love of God and neighbor is lost. I wonder if overly negative conceptions of holiness do not find their roots here. Likewise, when holiness is separated from realization of its "now, but not yet" nature—i.e., when the developmental nature of our becoming holy is lost—we too easily slide into an impatient judgmentalism. Perhaps we should recall that Wesley's order of salvation is just that: an *order*. There are steps and a progression to our move toward salvation, and there is to our growth in holiness as well. We do not expect a new convert to exhibit a mature level of holiness, though we do rightly expect all to be "going on to perfection." Similarly, mature Christians may sometimes fall. When this happens, our goal is restoration, not condemnation. By properly grasping the relationality implicit in the concept of holiness as well as its developmental nature, we stand best able to avoid these confusions.

Conclusion

We can see, now, how our misperceptions of either grace or holiness easily lead to the idea of a tension between the two. With the one error, serious failures to be holy are smiled at and indulged. With the other, we too easily become condemning and judgmental. When the two are rightly held in relation to each other, serious breaches of holiness by a brother or sister are met with a broken heart, and one of our first questions might well be whether we have contributed to the problem by failing the brother or sister in some way. This leads us neither to condemn nor to indulge, but rather to search for ways to reconciliation and restoration. That search is rooted in genuine love for the other that is, in turn, grounded in the recognition that humans cannot truly flourish apart from right relationship with God and neighbor. In short, it is our seeing the empowering nature of grace that leads us to extend precisely such grace to each other. We do not punish sin out of some retributive theory of justice; rather we insist on accountability as the first act of grace that is intended ultimately to lead to restoration and a return to the holiness that is manifested in the life that pleases God. Growth in holiness for the immature or restoration for one fallen—in neither case can I overemphasize the importance that an interaction be grounded in genuine love, not a self-righteousness that secretly exults in our own "superiority," not an ungodly curiosity that seeks titillation, not even a self-centeredness that seeks "notches" for our holiness belts, but rather a love that orients all actions toward the best interest of the other. To that end, I offer four suggestions for consideration.

First, genuine self-giving love ought never be confused with a condemnation disguised as "speaking the truth in love," when it really is more like "speaking harshness in self-righteousness." On the other hand, neither ought genuine love be confused with indulgence rooted in a fear of substantive or difficult dialogue. God extends grace to us freely and without regard to merit, but the fact that God intends grace to empower transformation means that there is a certain accountability that accompanies our reception of grace. Neither point can be forgotten.

Second, we ought never to confuse our role with that of the Holy Spirit. Too often, we overestimate our grasp of another's efforts and motivations, and we tend to think that we are able to "see things as they are," which enables us to speak challenging words to another. Of motivations, we know little, and our focus ought always to be on invocation of the Spirit. In short, we should not think we know more than we do.

Third, the "without regard to merit" aspect of God's bestowing grace should never be minimized. While, as I have argued, this may not be the primary aspect of God's grace, once we lose sight of it, we tend to think that others ought not "get more than they deserve." None of us are worthy of the grace we receive, and I can hardly imagine a greater failure than, after having received grace ourselves, to fail to be gracious to others.

Last, it is good to recall the old adage: Love the sinner, hate the sin. Our critical natures, coupled with our own doubts and fears, often lead us to a harsh self-righteousness that fails properly to recognize that: "There, but for the grace of God, go I."

Underlying the entirety of this essay has been an effort to focus our attention on the empowering nature of grace, specifically empowering us for holiness. May we all be the recipients of and witnesses to that grace that empowers us to live the life that makes God smile!

NOTES

Introduction: In Response to Grace

1. Frank Tillepaugh, *Unleashing the Church* (Ventura, Calif.: Regal, 1982), 59-62.

2. William J. Abraham, *The Logic of Evangelism* (Grand Rapids: Eerdmans, 1989), 13.

3. *The Works of John Wesley*, Bicentennial ed. (Nashville: Abingdon Press, 1984–), 9:527.

1. Apostolic and Postmodern Christianity

1. Stephen L. Carter, *The Culture of Disbelief: How American Law and Politics Trivialize Religious Devotion* (New York: Basic, 1993).

2. John M. G. Barclay, *Jews in the Mediterranean Diaspora: From Alexander to Trajan (333 B.C.E.–117 C.E.)* (Edinburgh: T & T Clark, 1996), 92-98.

3. See Max Turner, *Power from on High: The Spirit in Israel's Restoration and Witness in Luke–Acts* (Journal of Pentecostal Theology Supplement Series 9; Sheffield: Sheffield Academic Press, 1996).

4. See especially Matthias Wenk, *Community-forming Power: The Socio-Ethical Role of the Spirit in Luke–Acts* (Journal of Pentecostal Theology Supplement Series 19; Sheffield: Sheffield Academic Press, 2000), 259-73.

5. Rachel Zoll, "*Seventeen:* Fashion, Bible, Magazine Breaks Mold, Launches Section on Faith," *Lexington Herald-Leader* (11 September 2004): H1.

6. "We've a Story to Tell to the Nations," from *The United Methodist Hymnal* (Nashville: The United Methodist Publishing House, 1989), 569.

2. The Church and Change: What Can We Learn from Other Historic Transitions?

1. "The State of World Evangelization," http://www.missionfrontiers.org/newslinks/statewe.htm (accessed 6 November 2005).

2. Justo L. González, "Globalization in the Teaching of Church History," *Theological Education* 39, no. 2 (1993): 51.

3. According to Maximus of Tyre, some 30,000 deities could be identified around the Mediterranean area.

4. Samuel Hugh Moffett, A *History of Christianity in Asia*, vol. 1 (Maryknoll: Orbis, 1998), xiii-xv. Moffett notes that Asia produced the first known church building (Dura Europos), the first New Testament translation (Syriac, in 180 C.E.), perhaps the first Christian king, the first Christian poets, and even arguably the first Christian state. The message of ancient and apostolic Asian Christians developed apart from the distortions of Western Greek philosophy.

5. Candidates for baptism were questioned by a quick summary of Christian doctrine, based upon the baptismal formula of Matt 28:19, beginning with the question, "Do you believe in the Father, Son, and Holy Spirit?" Soon, several affirmations were added to ensure that the candidate affirmed the right beliefs. These affirmations were called the Rule of Faith, and were used against heresies. Spurred on by heresies, especially Marcion (and his own canon), the Christians needed to define what the true limits of the Bible were. The Greek word *kanōn* literally means "straight rod," "bar," or "rule used by masons and carpenters," and so the "rule" by which the authentic books of the apostles would be known (thus helping to ensure the apostolicity of the church).

6. Paul G. Schrotenboer, "The Church and Higher Education," *Theological Forum* 20, no. 4 (1992): 3; http://www.gospelcom.net/rec/TF-Dec92Schrotenboer.html (accessed 1 November 2004).

7. Historically, Armenia is the first national church, declared thus by King Tiridates III in 301 C.E. The Armenian Church celebrated its 1,700th anniversary in 2001.

8. Theodotius, who made Christianity the only official religion, was more "Constantinian" than Constantine; see J. Denny Weaver, *The Nonviolent Atonement* (Grand Rapids: Eerdmans, 2001), 83. See Richard E. Rubenstein, *When Jesus Became God: The Struggle to Define Christianity during the Last Days of Rome* (San Diego: Harcourt, 2000).

9. Roger Olson, *The Story of Christian Theology* (Downers Grove: InterVarsity Press, 1999), 157.

10. Bernard McGinn, *The Growth of Mysticism* (New York: Crossroads, 1994), 150.

11. Regarding this period, Kenneth Scott Latourette comments, "The trend towards regarding the Popes as the successors of the Caesars and the papacy as the exponent and protector of *Romanitas* brought both beneficent results and perils. On the one hand, it gave to the Church of the West a structural unity, helped to hold Europe together, and made for civilization. On the other, it substituted . . . visible organizational unity for the unity of love and mixed the kind of power represented by the Roman Empire with that of the Cross and resurrection. The latter was not completely lost, but it suffered by its conjunction with *Romanitas*" (*A History of Christianity*, vol. 1 [New York: HarperCollins, 1975], 340).

12. Augustine established near the cathedral in his own house a *monasterium clericorum* (a clergy house rather than a seminary), and in only a few years produced ten bishops for various sees in Africa.

13. Scholasticism designates a particular approach to Christian theology. Dated from 1100–1500, it suggests a theological method associated with organized textbook theology and the thesis method.

14. Kevin Word, "Africa," in *A World History of Christianity*, ed. Adrian Hastings (London: Cassell, 1999), 194.

15. Steven Ozmont, *The Age of Reform: 1250–1550* (New Haven: Yale University Press, 1981).

16. Mark A. Noll, ed., *Confessions and Catechisms of the Reformation* (Grand Rapids: Baker, 1991).

17. Schrotenboer, "Church and Higher Education," 4. At the time of Calvin's death, his Geneva Academy (seminary) had about 1,200 students, drawn from all of Europe.

18. "The notion of the Word of God as Jesus Christ himself allowed Luther to respond to one of the main objections Catholics raised to his doctrine of the authority of Scripture above the church. . . . Luther responded that it was neither the church, but the gospel, Jesus Christ, that had made both the Bible and the church. Final authority rests neither in the church nor in the Bible, but in the gospel, in the message of Jesus Christ, who is the incarnate Word of God. Since Scripture gives a more trustworthy witness to the gospel than the pope's corrupt church, or even the best in Christian tradition, the Bible has authority over church, pope, and tradition" (Justo L. González, *The Story of Christianity*, vol. 2 [New York: HarperCollins, 1985], 31).

19. Thomas C. Oden, *Systematic Theology*, 3 vols. (San Francisco: HarperSanFrancisco, 1987–1994), 323.

20. James Wm. McClendon Jr., with Nancey Murphy, "Witness" vol. 3 of *Systematic Theology* (Nashville: Abingdon Press, 2000), 221-24.

21. I am using *evangelical* in a broad and loose sense—cf. Donald W. Dayton and Robert K. Johnston, *The Variety of American Evangelicalism* (Downers Grove, Ill.: InterVarsity Press, 1991); also Donald W. Dayton, "The Search for the Historical Evangelicalism: George Marsden's History of Fuller Seminary as a Case Study," *Christian Scholars Review* 23 (1993): 12-33.

22. See Mark A. Noll, "The Rise of Evangelicalism: The Age of Edwards, Whitefield and the Wesleys," vol. 1 of *A History of Evangelicalism: People, Movements and Ideas in the English-Speaking World* (Downers Grove, Ill.: InterVarsity Press, 2003).

23. Leonard Sweet, *Aquachurch: Essential Leadership Arts for Piloting Your Church in Today's Fluid Culture* (Loveland, Colo.: Vital, 1999), 24.

24. "For the first time in history, there are fewer non-Christians within the unreached peoples than there are within the reached groups. . . . We are in the final era of missions. For the first time in history we can anticipate the completions (sic) of the missionary task, which is to establish an indigenous church planting movement within the language and social structure of every people on earth" ("State of World Evangelism," http://www.missionfrontiers.org/newslinks/statewe.htm).

25. Philip Jenkins, *The Next Christendom: The Coming of Global Christianity* (Oxford: Oxford University Press, 2002). By 2050, only about one-fifth of the world's three billion Christians will be non-Hispanic whites.

26. Ibid., 11.

27. John David Walt, "The New Christendom," Web Parish (www.asbury blog.net; accessed 3 May 2004).

28. See Ronald J. Sider, *Rich Christians in an Age of Hunger* (Nashville: Word, 1997).

29. Alister E. McGrath, *The Future of Christianity* (Oxford: Blackwell, 2002), 79-82.

30. Philip Jenkins, "Globalization and the Transformation of Christianity," *Watch on the West* 3, no. 1 (2002): 4.

31. David B. Barrett et al., eds., *World Christian Encyclopedia*, vol. 1 (Oxford: Oxford University Press, 2001), 10. "Independent" refers to African independent churches, Chinese house churches, Latin American churches, and so on.

32. Pablo A. Deiros, "The Roots and Fruits of the Argentine Revival," in *The Rising Revival*, eds. C. Peter Wagner and Pablo Deiros (Ventura, Calif.: Gospel Light, 1998), 53.

33. McGinn, *Growth of Mysticism*, 152-53.

34. Reggie McNeal, *Revolution in Leadership: Training Apostles for Tomorrow's Church* (Nashville: Abingdon Press, 1998).

35. Michael S. Hamilton and Jennifer McKinney, "Turning the Mainline Around," http://www.christianitytoday.com/ct/2003/008/1.34.html (accessed 6 November 2004).

36. Cecil Sherman, the former coordinator of the Cooperative Baptist Fellowship, discounts postdenominationalism, arguing that denominations may change but will not go away (Mark Wingfield, "Sherman Says New Convention Is Coming," http://www.baptiststandard.com/2002/7_1/print/cbf_sherman.html [accessed 1 July 2002]).

37. Oden, *Systematic Theology*, 2:21.

38. John Wesley, "Letters," vol. 13 in *The Works of John Wesley*, 3rd ed. (Grand Rapids: Baker, 1986), 258.

39. Justo L. González, *The Changing Shape of Church History* (St. Louis: Chalice Press, 2002), 151-54. One of González's major visions for the future of church history is one of incarnational marginality: "When I speak of incarnate marginality, what I mean above all is that Christians must acknowledge that our proper place, both as individuals and as the church, is not necessarily at the center. Without condemning Eusebius or Constantine, without declaring the entire Middle Ages apostate, without rejecting the inheritance that we have received from so many centuries of official and extraofficial support by the state and society at large, we must affirm that the proper place for those who follow Jesus Christ is the margin rather than the center; it is the valley rather than the hilltop; it is the cross rather than the throne" [153].

3. Grace in a Postmodern World

1. For greater detail about these aspects of grace, please refer to my book, *The Way to Heaven: The Gospel According to John Wesley* (Grand Rapids: Zondervan, 2003). More broadly, see Paul Chilcote, ed., *The Wesleyan Tradition: A Paradigm for Renewal* (Nashville: Abingdon Press, 2002); Kenneth J. Collins, *The Scripture Way of Salvation: The Heart of John Wesley's Theology* (Nashville: Abingdon Press, 1997); David L. McKenna, *What a Time to Be Wesleyan!* (Kansas City: Beacon Hill, 1999); Al Truesdale and Bonnie Perry, *A Dangerous Hope: Encountering the God of Grace* (Kansas City: Beacon Hill, 1997).

2. I make this emphasis because there are some who believe that postmodernism is an imposition upon a cultural reality rather than a reflection of it. While I may not use the term *postmodernism* as some do, to create as a wide gap between life today and life in times past, I nevertheless believe

that postmodernity is real and that we have to deal with its chief defining characteristics. In the spirit of Charles Wesley, we must "serve the present age."

3. I refer to the elements of "the postmodern ethos" identified in Stanley Grenz, ch. 2 of A Primer on Postmodernism (Grand Rapids: Eerdmans, 1996). See also George G. Hunter III, Radical Outreach (Nashville: Abingdon Press, 2003); Jeremy Langford, God Moments: Why Faith Really Matters to a New Generation (Maryknoll: Orbis, 2001); Leonard Sweet, Post-Modern Pilgrims (Nashville: Broadman-Holman, 2000); Robert Tuttle, Can We Talk? Sharing Your Faith in a Pre-Christian World (Nashville: Abingdon Press, 1999).

4. Stephen Seamands has dealt with this well in his book, Wounds That Heal: Bringing Our Hurts to the Cross (Downers Grove, Ill.: InterVarsity Press, 2003).

5. Philip Yancey, What's So Amazing about Grace? (Grand Rapids: Zondervan, 1997), 11.

6. This is precisely what a growing number of renewal authors are saying today, including the challenging book by Bill Easum, Put On Your Own Oxygen Mask First (Nashville: Abingdon Press, 2004).

7. See George G. Hunter III, The Celtic Way of Evangelism (Nashville: Abingdon Press, 2000), 52-55, for an overview of how this new missional paradigm has developed.

8. Everett M. Rogers is a contemporary writer on the subject of assimilation. His book, Diffusion of Innovations, 4th ed. (New York: Free, 1995), describes six essential steps in the assimilation of an idea: awareness, interest, relevance, trial, adoption, and reinforcement. Every one of these features can be identified in the early Methodist system of Societies, Classes, and Bands.

9. Eugene Peterson, The Contemplative Pastor (Dallas: Word, 1989), p. 11.

4. Holiness of Heart and Life in a Postmodern World

1. John Wesley, Explanatory Notes on the Old Testament, note on Genesis 1:28.

2. John Wesley, Sermon 51, "The Good Steward." Cf. Wesley on Luke 16:1, Explanatory Notes on the New Testament. Wesley is here of course using "man" in the inclusive sense of "all humankind," men and women.

3. Sandra Richter, "Stewardship of the Environment: A Christian Value," unpublished paper, Asbury Theological Seminary, 2004.

4. Creation Care is the name of the quarterly magazine of the Evangelical Environmental Network (www.creationcare.org).

5. The call to Noah is a call to and promise of preservation of the earth, and thus reinforces the call to earth stewardship.

6. This is of course a distortion of biblical missional ecclesiology, which in the person of Jesus Christ and the Holy Spirit is always linked with the kingdom of God.

7. John Wesley, *Explanatory Notes upon the New Testament*, on Matt 6:10.

8. The kingdom call may be seen as part of the call to peoplehood, as suggested for instance by Exodus 19, 1 Peter 2, and many other passages. But because Christian theology (both popular and academic) in the West, especially, tends to drive a wedge between church and kingdom, we today in our contemporary context get a more faithful understanding of God's call by making the kingdom call explicit.

9. Glen H. Stassen and David P. Gushee, *Kingdom Ethics: Following Jesus in Contemporary Context* (Downers Grove, Ill.: InterVarsity Press, 2003).

10. This is true for Christians everywhere, but especially for those in contexts where ethnic pride or national identity threatens to compromise kingdom allegiance.

11. In my book *Kingdom, Church, and World* (Eugene, Ore.: Wipf & Stock, 2001), I show how the biblical kingdom of God theme ties together many other biblical themes, including *shalom*, sabbath, jubilee, land, justice for the poor, and city of God.

12. It is clear from this as well as the larger biblical context that "poor," "captives," and "oppressed" here include all forms of poverty, bondage, and oppression (Luke 4:18-19). The terms should not be limited either to exclusively spiritual or to solely political or socioeconomic categories.

13. Howard A. Snyder, *The Community of the King*, rev. ed. (Downers Grove, Ill.: InterVarsity Press, 2004).

14. As Peter, John, Paul, and other New Testament writers emphasized—e.g., Philippians 2:1-15; 1 Peter 2:21-23; 1 John 2:6.

15. The biblical doctrine of stewardship is based on two interrelated principles: responsible care for the entirety of the material world entrusted to humankind (including time, money, and the physical environment), and responsible stewardship of God's "manifold grace" (1 Pet 4:10). By the Spirit, God grants us "supernatural" grace as the necessary resource for his people to be good stewards of the "natural" world.

16. This was of course a key discovery of John Wesley and the early Methodists as they developed the community and discipling structures of Society, Class, and Band.

17. E. Stanley Jones, *Christ's Alternative to Communism* (New York: Abingdon Press, 1935); E. Stanley Jones, *Is the Kingdom of God Realism?* (New York: Abingdon Press, 1940).

18. Today's stress on gradual growth and on character and moral development is helpful. I largely agree with the critique that the nineteenth-century holiness movement at times overemphasized crisis and underplayed process in the work of sanctification, particularly in some branches of the movement. Today perhaps we may face the opposite danger of overemphasizing process, either in reaction to Pentecostal/Charismatic emphases or in reaction to our own history. It would be un-Wesleyan as well as unbiblical to lose the crisis/process nexus.

19. Holiness is the opposite of what the Bible calls being "doubleminded" (e.g., Jas 1:7).

5. The Priesthood of All Believers in the Postmodern Congregation

1. R. Paul Stevens, *The Other Six Days* (Grand Rapids: Eerdmans, 1999), 173-75.

2. Edward Schillebeeckx, *Ministry: Leadership* (Edinburgh: T & T Clark, 1999), 70.

3. Richard E. Leakey, *People of the Lake: Mankind and Its Beginnings* (New York: Doubleday, 1978).

4. Augustine, *City of God*, 20.10.729.

5. Martin Luther, *Works*, 1:316.

6. Ibid., 2:282-83.

7. Ibid., 2:282.

8. Ibid., 36:106-7.

9. Robert Southey, *The Life of Wesley; and Rise and Progress of Methodism*, vol. 1 (London: Longman, Brown, Green, and Longmans, 1846), 333.

10. Ibid., 334.

11. In 1866 the Methodist Episcopal Church South held a General Conference in New Orleans and in one day abandoned the itineracy, compulsory class attendance, and probationary membership, in effect undermining its strong lay base. Some believe that at that moment the Methodist Episcopal Church South ceased to be a movement of the Spirit.

12. Sue Mallory, *The Equipping Church* (Grand Rapids: Zondervan, 2001), 198-99.

CONTRIBUTORS

Meesaeng Lee Choi is Associate Professor of Church History at Asbury Theological Seminary.

Joel B. Green is Professor of New Testament Interpretation at Asbury Theological Seminary.

Jeffrey E. Greenway is Senior Pastor of Reynoldsburg United Methodist Church in Reynoldsburg, Ohio.

Charles E. Gutenson is Associate Professor of Philosophical Theology at Asbury Theological Seminary.

Steve Harper is Vice President of Asbury Theological Seminary, Florida Campus.

Howard A. Snyder recently retired as Professor of History and Theology of Mission at Asbury Theological Seminary.

Robert G. Tuttle Jr. is Professor of Evangelism at Asbury Theological Seminary.